Dr. Benny Tate is always encouraging in his teaching. It is simple enough for me to understand. I love this new book! He shows us that we are all leaders—we all have influence. Is our influence negative or positive? I want to be a positive leader; this book shows me how. Buy it. Read it. Apply its truths, and you will become the leader you always wanted to be.

—RUTH GRAHAM
DAUGHTER OF REV. BILLY GRAHAM; FOUNDER, RUTH GRAHAM AND FRIENDS; AUTHOR; SPEAKER

Benny Tate reminds us that God is a "yes, you can" God. Human nature is can't-do, but God's nature is can-do, and He sees in every person something that nobody else can see. Benny writes from his personal experience of how saying yes to God opens a future of hope. Read this book and see how your life can also experience "yes, you can."

—DR. JOHN ED MATHISON
FOUNDER, JOHN ED MATHISON LEADERSHIP MINISTRIES

As someone who plays to win because I refuse to lose, Benny Tate's book *Yes, You Can* is a hands-on tool to help you win in life! Anyone anywhere can apply these winning strategies to make a lasting impact. I tell my players: "If you're not willing to lead, then you're not ready for what's next." Whether it's in the NBA or in life, leadership is the difference between being good and being great. *Yes, You Can* will give you the tools you need to lead!

COACH, UNIVERSITY OF ARKANS

Pastor Benny Tate has been the leading light for so many people. His dedication to his faith and gift to lead through the Lord is not just impressive but needed. In this book he motivates us to see that God's belief in what we can do is much greater than what we can imagine. I am thankful to call Pastor Benny a friend and thankful for him making a difference in my life!

—Ryan Ridder
Head Coach, Mercer University Men's Basketball

Many good people have written excellent books on theories of leadership. But they have very little experience in leading any entity themselves. Dr. Benny Tate gives us an excellent volume from one who has and is actually leading. In this book theory comes from actual practice. Dr. Tate leads one of the most exciting, fastest-growing churches in America. From leading oneself to leading others, Brother Benny covers the ground in productive ways. You will be blessed, helped, and challenged by *Yes, You Can*!

—Jerry Vines
Pastor Emeritus, First Baptist Church,
Jacksonville, Florida
Two-Time President, the Southern Baptist Convention

# YES, YOU CAN

**BENNY TATE**

with **STACEY HENSLEY**

CHARISMA
HOUSE

Yes, You Can by Benny Tate
Published by Charisma House, an imprint of Charisma Media
1150 Greenwood Blvd., Lake Mary, Florida 32746

Copyright © 2025 by Benny Tate. All rights reserved.

Unless otherwise noted, all Scripture quotations are taken from The ESV® Bible (The Holy Bible, English Standard Version®), copyright © 2001 by Crossway, a publishing ministry of Good News Publishers. Used by permission. All rights reserved.

Scripture quotations marked kjv are from the King James Version of the Bible.

Scripture quotations marked nasb are taken from the (NASB®) New American Standard Bible®, Copyright © 1960, 1971, 1977, 1995, 2020 by The Lockman Foundation. Used by permission. All rights reserved. www.lockman.org

Scripture quotations marked niv are taken from the Holy Bible, New International Version®, NIV®. Copyright © 1973, 1978, 1984, 2011 by Biblica, Inc.® Used by permission of Zondervan. All rights reserved worldwide. www.zondervan.com. The "NIV" and "New International Version" are trademarks registered in the United States Patent and Trademark Office by Biblica, Inc.®

While the author has made every effort to provide accurate, up-to-date source information at the time of publication, statistics and other data are constantly updated. Neither the publisher nor the author assumes any responsibility for errors or for changes that occur after publication. Further, the publisher and author do not have any control over and do not assume any responsibility for third-party websites or their content.

For more resources like this, visit MyCharismaShop.com and the author's website at www.rockspringsonline.com/benny-tate/.

Cataloging-in-Publication Data is on file with the Library of Congress.

International Standard Book Number: 978-1-63641-457-7

E-book ISBN: 978-1-63641-458-4

1 2025

Printed in the United States of America

Most Charisma Media products are available at special quantity discounts for bulk purchase for sales promotions, premiums, fund-raising, and educational needs. For details, call us at (407) 333-0600 or visit our website at charismamedia.com.

# DEDICATION

*I lovingly dedicate this book to Dr. Clayton Jones. Ecclesiastes 11:1 tells us, "Cast your bread upon the waters, for you will find it after many days." I've had the privilege of watching that Scripture come to life in my own journey.*

*Forty-four years ago, Dr. Jones came to my home—at midnight—and led a searching, unsure sixteen-year-old boy to faith in Jesus Christ. He saw value in someone who seemingly had little to offer. But the bread he cast that night did return.*

*Decades later, I had the humbling honor of preaching at Tracy City Methodist Church in Tennessee, where another sixteen-year-old man gave his life to Jesus. His name was Logan Jones—the grandson of Dr. Clayton Jones.*

*Dr. Jones, you may never fully grasp the reach of your obedience this side of heaven. But I can tell you with certainty: Your faithfulness has echoed through generations.*

*Thank you for seeing me, believing in me, and pointing me to the One who changed everything.*

# CONTENTS

*Foreword by Anne Beiler* ............................. xi
*Introduction* ......................................... xiii

## PART I:
### LEADING YOURSELF FIRST

Chapter 1: Yes, You Were Created to Lead ............... 3
Chapter 2: Yes, You Should Have Time Alone
    with God ......................................... 11
Chapter 3: Yes, Discipline Is Your Friend ............... 23
Chapter 4: Yes, You Were Created on Purpose
    for a Purpose .................................... 31

## PART II:
### LEADING THOSE WHO WALK BESIDE YOU

Chapter 5: Yes, Leadership Is Serving Others ........... 43
Chapter 6: Yes, You Can Encourage Others ............. 53
Chapter 7: Yes, You Should Prefer Others ............... 65

## PART III:
### LEADING THOSE YOU SERVE

Chapter 8: Yes, Humility Is Required ................... 75
Chapter 9: Yes, Mindset Matters ....................... 83
Chapter 10: Yes, Priorities Matter ..................... 97

## PART IV:
### LEADING THOSE ENTRUSTED TO YOUR CARE

Chapter 11: Yes, You Should Cast a Clear Vision ....... 107
Chapter 12: Yes, You Can Empower Others ............ 115
Chapter 13: Yes, You Can Lead by Being Present ....... 125
Chapter 14: Yes, You Can Change ..................... 131

## PART V:
**LEADING WHEN LIFE IS HARD**

Chapter 15: Yes, You Can Lead When Life Is Hard ..... 141
Chapter 16: Yes, You Can Recover from
    Discouragement ..............................151
Chapter 17: Yes, You Can Overcome Insecurity ........ 157

## PART VI:
**INSPIRED TO LEAD? WHAT DO I DO NEXT?**

Chapter 18: Yes, You Can Continue to Grow........... 165
Chapter 19: Yes, You Can Be Generous................. 175
Chapter 20: Yes, Testing Can Affirm Your Call to Lead... 183

Conclusion: Does Leadership Really Matter?.......... 191
A Personal Invitation from the Author .............. 195
Appendix............................................. 197
Acknowledgments...................................... 199
Notes ............................................... 201
About the Author .................................... 205

# FOREWORD

Pastor Benny has written this book to encourage you that "you matter."

As you read this book it will be crystal clear that each of us are created with a specific purpose to fulfill as we fill up space on planet earth. When you know your life was planned on purpose by God, you will always know "life is an adventure." Simply reading the chapter titles of this book will inspire you to become "more."

Benny has a way of making the impossible seem possible and declares, "*All* things are possible."

His story is a testimony of what one person can do by saying, "Yes, I can."

If you're stuck or the mountain in front of you seems impossible to climb, start climbing and with each step say, "Yes, I can."

—Anne Beiler
Founder, Auntie Anne's

# INTRODUCTION

In my book *Defy the Odds* I shared my story and how we can have hope despite our circumstances. In *Unlimited* I showed how to better understand the Holy Spirit and how His work in our lives can give abounding hope in Jesus and abiding peace in our hearts. The book you're holding now, *Yes, You Can!*, is what happens when we indeed defy the odds, embrace and harness the unlimited power of the Holy Spirit, and realize that, yes, we can be good leaders among those God has put in our lives—and have extraordinary impact for God's glory!

In the early days of my ministry, I married Barbara and pastored a church part-time earning three hundred dollars per month. I also worked in a machine shop to supplement our income, but I felt the Lord calling me to preach full-time. Where I was from, pastors worked additional jobs because we rarely made enough money preaching to provide for our families.

When I went home to tell Barbara that I had decided to stop working another job just to pay bills, Barbara said, "I don't know how, but I believe the Lord must be leading you." I replied, "Maybe if I go full-time, the church will pay me more. And other churches may invite me to lead revivals, and we can make enough money to live on."

I felt that God had something bigger for my life. I wanted my life to count for Him.

I believe the Lord wants something bigger for your life too!

Not long after we decided that I should preach fulltime, I told Barbara I felt the Lord was also calling me to take college classes. Again, where we are from, people were against preachers having any type of formal education. They believed that if God calls you, you do not need man's influence, and there is no reason to get more education. I started going to school secretly, not wanting anyone to know what I was doing. All along, I sensed that God had something big for my life.

He certainly did! And I want you to know, God has something big for *your* life—bigger than you can imagine. As Ephesians 3:20 says, "Now to him who is able to do *far more abundantly than all that we ask or think*, according to the power at work within us" (emphasis added).

You may be one who has been told your entire life, "No" or "You can't." You may have been told you were not chosen for a job or a team. You may have been told you were not worth staying around for. What if just *one time* you were told, "Yes, you can"?

Well, I'm saying it. Yes, you can!

Roger Bannister was told no one would ever break a four-minute mile. But in 1954, at age twenty-five, he ran the mile in 3:59.4. Then, because he had broken that record, other runners began believing that they could too. Today more than eighteen hundred athletes have been able to run a sub-four-minute mile.

I want you to know that no matter your background, no matter what you've been told you can or cannot do,

*Introduction*

no matter your circumstances and what challenges you face, yes, you can. You can lead others effectively. You can lead your home. You can lead your children. You can lead others in your workplace. You can lead a ministry or church. God wants you to have a full life in Him!

In this book I will not talk about CEO leadership. I will share about "unlikely" people today and in Scripture whom God has used to do extraordinary things! I will share a treasure house of proven strategies from the world's all-time best leadership book—God's Word—and from what I've learned (sometimes the hard way!) since my life-changing decision. My mission in this book is to encourage and equip you to graciously lead your life, your family, your boss, and those around you. Leading is serving and caring for those with whom you have influence, and you were created to lead!

The Bible is full of examples of how people from unlikely backgrounds became effective leaders. God used the apostle Paul, who had been arresting followers of Christ. God also used a tax-collector who worked for the Roman government, an anti-Rome zealot, and uneducated fishermen to take His message to all the world.

God also used people like Jephthah. This is how Judges 11:1 describes him: "Now Jephthah the Gileadite was a mighty warrior, but he was the son of a prostitute." Notice the description: "a mighty warrior" who was "the son of a prostitute." I can understand how Jephthah felt. I was told by one of my stepfathers that I was not good enough for the family, and I did not know my biological father until I was thirty years old. When you go on to read Judges 11, you find that Jephthah was thrown out of his father's house by his half-brothers because they were the sons of Gilead's wife. But do you know what God did? He used Jephthah to save the nation of Israel from the Ammonites.

If God can use Paul, Matthew, a band of uneducated Jewish fishermen, and Jephthah—and an unlikely part-time pastor named Benny Tate—to step up and lead those around them to accomplish His will, then yes, He can use you too!

"But God chose what is foolish in the world to shame the wise," Paul wrote in 1 Corinthians 1:27–29. "God chose what is weak in the world to shame the strong; God chose what is low and despised in the world, even things that are not, to bring to nothing things that are, so that no human being might boast in the presence of God."

If you are breathing, you have influence over someone. If you have influence over anyone, you can care for them. If you can care for and influence people, you are a leader! My prayer is that *Yes, You Can!* will ignite within you the same hope, inspiration, encouragement, and practical strategies I've discovered in my life. Indeed, God uses the "unlikely" people to do extraordinary work for Him. If you have any influence with anyone in any capacity, He can use you too.

Want to become a good leader? A better leader? A person of significant, positive influence? Yes, you can!

## PART I

# LEADING YOURSELF FIRST

*For we are his workmanship, created in Christ Jesus for good works.*
—**Ephesians 2:10**

CHAPTER 1

# YES, YOU WERE CREATED TO LEAD

I BELIEVED EARLY ON that God had something special for my life, and I strongly believe He has something special for your life too. You are His workmanship, and that means you are His masterpiece. God created the sky, stars, galaxies, water, vegetation, and animals, and when He finished, He "saw that it was good" (Genesis 1:10). But when God created mankind, which includes you and me, "God saw everything that he had made, and behold, it was *very* good" (Genesis 1:31, emphasis added).

As God's workmanship created by His hand, we were given responsibilities by Him. His Word tells us that God created us to "rule over" or "have dominion over" the world He has made. In Genesis 1:28, God told Adam and Eve to "have dominion over the fish of the sea and over the birds of the heavens and over every living thing that moves on the earth." The words "over every" in this verse mean "the whole...(hence), all, any or every."[1]

God created you and me to *lead*! In Genesis 2:15 we read, "The LORD God took the man and put him in the garden of Eden to work it and keep it." God was telling Adam that He was placing him in the garden, and he was to work, serve, nurture, and guard the garden. God intended the people He created to lead and serve over His creation. There were no specific guidelines, no books to read, no seminars to attend. God told Adam and Eve to do what they were created to do: to have dominion over, to lead.

Today we often seek leaders who are already leading. We look at those who are moving up in a corporation or who appear to have already arrived. We look up to people who have titles in a business or lead a large church or organization and naturally regard them as leaders because they are at the top of their game or earn big paychecks. I'm not saying such people aren't leaders; what I'm saying is that you are too!

We often compare ourselves to such people and mistakenly think we are not leaders or that we're not capable of leading. All through the Scriptures, God shows us that we can lead, no matter who or where we are. He's given us dozens of confidence-boosting examples of how ordinary men and women became extraordinary leaders by walking closely with Him.

We must understand that, as He did in biblical times, God calls us to lead wherever He has planted us. He has planted some of us in business. He has put us at desks or at home with the kids. He may have us taking care of parents or driving trucks. We may be fixing powerlines for power companies or picking up trash or working in a hospital or government job. God put Adam and Eve in a garden, and they messed up that assignment. They were not obedient and ate from the only tree He told them not to eat from. There were consequences to their decision, and He moved them outside the garden. From that moment forward, Eve was told that childbearing would be hard, and Adam was told that he would work the ground and it would be difficult. (See Genesis 3:16–19.) God tells us we can and should lead, no matter who we are or what our background is. He grants us all the capacity to lead right where He plants us. God puts unlikely people in places to do extraordinary work for His perfect will.

Let me tell you what I mean.

I love Nehemiah because he is one of the most overlooked leaders in the Bible. He was not ordained, nor was he a prophet or priest. His job was that of a cupbearer working for Artaxerxes, the Persian king. The cupbearer was not a prestigious role. His job was to take the first drink from the king's cup to see if it had been poisoned. If the cupbearer did not die, then the king knew it was safe to drink from the cup. So, in three simple words, Nehemiah was expendable. If Nehemiah died, that was fine. The important thing was that the king didn't die. Nehemiah was expendable—to everybody but God!

**GOD PUTS UNLIKELY PEOPLE IN PLACES TO DO EXTRAORDINARY WORK FOR HIS PERFECT WILL.**

You may feel that you are expendable or that you don't matter—like you're a cupbearer. You may feel that your income or your position in the workplace determines your worth. I understand. As I was growing up, I played sports. I remember one Saturday practice that ended at noon, and my mama and stepdad had told me they would come back to get me. I waited and waited and waited. It started getting dark, and I was still there waiting. Finally, one of my parents pulled up and said, "We just forgot about you." That was my life. As I've grown older and close to God through Jesus Christ, I've taken great comfort in the fact that I matter to God. This is what I want you to know: You matter to God. You are His creation, made in His image. He loves you and He cares deeply about you.

If you know Christ as your Savior and Lord, you are God's child. What's amazing about Nehemiah is that he approached King Artaxerxes about the wall of Jerusalem being in disarray, and the king allowed him to return to Jerusalem, purchase what he needed, and lead people in rebuilding the wall in just fifty-two days (Nehemiah 6:15)! The guy who was expendable in the king's court went on to accomplish important things for God!

Nehemiah shows us what leadership is: serving and caring for other people. During the Babylonian invasion of Judah, Jerusalem's wall had been destroyed. Babylon had taken the strongest, smartest, and best-looking Jewish people captive and left others behind in Judah. Subsequently, Persia defeated Babylon, and many of the Judean hostages were taken to Persia. This is where Nehemiah became cupbearer to King Artaxerxes. Eventually, visitors from Jerusalem brought news that the people in Jerusalem were in great distress, the wall remained in ruins, and the city gates had not been rebuilt. Jerusalem was not safe, and the people were extremely worried. Nehemiah was heartbroken. "As soon as I heard these words I sat down and wept and mourned for days" (Nehemiah 1:4). He cared for his people.

Often, a leader will step up and lead from his or her greatest hurt. I can tell you that has been true for me. There have been times when I was made fun of for my accent. I spent nights falling asleep practicing how to say words like *fire* and *tire*. In my early days as a pastor, I didn't have enough money to buy books, so I would watch Billy Graham to get a free book at the end of his message. I also made frequent trips to the library to check out books so I could increase my learning. I never enrolled in a college, so I earned my degree through correspondence, mailing my work in.

But see how God has worked through these challenges: I certainly do not make fun of anyone with an accent. But more importantly, when people visit our church or watch online, it is sometimes *because of* my accent! I want everyone to be able to have a book, so I price my books so people can afford one. I made sure my daughter, Savannah Abigail, was able to go to college, and now she has her doctorate. God has accomplished so much more through me than I ever could have accomplished on my own. He has allowed me to experience challenges and hurts so that my heart for people stays tender and I can better care for them. That is leadership—caring for those with whom God allows me to have influence.

**THAT IS LEADERSHIP— CARING FOR THOSE WITH WHOM GOD ALLOWS ME TO HAVE INFLUENCE.**

Have you ever considered that you were created to lead? Be very honest with yourself. What is holding you back from leading your family? Please do not use the excuse that your spouse will not let you. Leadership is all about care and influence.

What is keeping you from being a leader where you work? You could say that your boss has overlooked you for promotion. You might think you don't want to invest the time, expense, and hassle of getting management training in hopes of being promoted. And that's fine. How can you best care for and influence those around you? What can you do to lead in those ways where you are right now?

Yes, you can lead where you are, just as you are—and make a world of difference!

Here's the first step: Lead yourself first. It is hard to care for and lead others if you do not prioritize caring for yourself. So our next three chapters will show how I've learned to first take care of myself in order to better lead my wife, family, staff, church, friends, and others. I call this "inward leadership." My prayer is that when you finish this book, you will fully embrace these life-changing truths.

You are important to God and to the people He has placed within your reach.

As you walk closely with Him and first take care of yourself, He will enable you to influence and care for the men, women, young people, and children of your life in ways that both edify them and glorify God.

You were created to lead.

He will create in you the confidence to lead well—wherever you are!

## FOR REFLECTION

1. In the beginning God gave Adam and Eve dominion over every living thing. How do you think they learned to lead without books to read or seminars to attend?

2. Do you see yourself as a leader? Why or why not?

3. Do you believe that anyone can lead regardless of their background or the challenges they face? Explain.

4. As God did for Nehemiah, has He given you a burden to correct a wrong or undertake a certain task? What have you done to pursue it?

5. Think about areas of hurt in your life. Have your hurts made you more empathetic toward others? In what ways?

## PRINCIPLES TO REMEMBER

- If you have influence over anyone in your life, God created you to lead.
- God uses the "unlikely" people to do extraordinary work for Him.
- Leadership is caring for those with whom God allows us to have influence.
- Before you can do anything, you must get *you* right.

## CHAPTER 2

# YES, YOU SHOULD HAVE TIME ALONE WITH GOD

Being inwardly sound is paramount for every leader. Being inwardly sound as a spouse, parent, employer, employee, pastor, or volunteer is paramount. I have found that there is only one way to get the peace you need to face the challenges of each new day, and that is time alone with God in prayer. The hardest person you will ever lead is yourself, and the only way to get yourself right is to go to God in prayer—regularly, daily. And there are days when you should pray second by second. As the apostle Paul wrote in 1 Thessalonians 5:17, we're to "pray without ceasing."

Prayer is essential to leading yourself first. I will tell you in full transparency that this has been one of the biggest battles of my life. I've had periods when I've done well and periods when I have not done well. It is a constant struggle because it's easy to become a slave to the needs of the immediate. The enemy prefers that we prepare the lesson more than we prepare ourselves.

**THE HARDEST PERSON YOU WILL EVER LEAD IS YOURSELF**

My greatest successes have come when I wake up and begin my day in prayer. I will tell you why I believe that praying in the morning is the right thing to do. I look at Jesus in Scripture: "And rising very early in the morning, while it was still dark, he departed and went out to a desolate place, and there he prayed" (Mark 1:35). Jesus went away alone to pray regularly. And I consider how David says, "O Lord, in the morning you hear my voice; in the morning I prepare a sacrifice for you and watch" (Psalm 5:3). Often in God's Word I am reminded that it is a best practice to wake up early and spend time with the Lord. To help remind me to pray early and often, I've even had a special rug made for my office that reads, "Have you prayed today?"

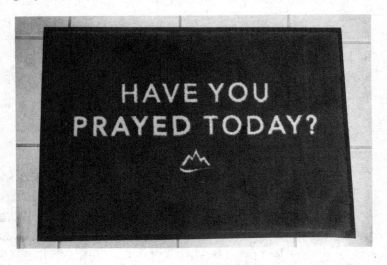

So I arrive in the morning and shut the door to my office first thing because if I don't first spend time alone with the Lord, people and tasks will start pulling at me. I begin by reading Scripture, then a devotional or book that directs my heart to the Lord. After several minutes of contemplative reading, I go to God in prayer. Sometimes

I pray and cry out to God because my heart is burdened. Other times I journal or write a letter to God.

You may ask how I pray. I've found that it helps my focus to pray through the simple acrostic you may be familiar with: ACTS.

**A: Adoration.** I begin my time of prayer praising the Lord. I praise Him for who He is and what He has done in my life, that He is the Creator, sustainer, peace, and truth in my life. I adore Him for saving my life, and I praise Him by faith for what He will do in my life during the coming day. As I pray in adoration of Him, I am comforted and strengthened by remembering who He is to me and who I am talking to. Adoration is a great way to remind myself that He is God and I am not. He is so worthy of our adoration!

**C: Confession.** Next, I spend time confessing any unconfessed sin to God and asking His forgiveness. I am specific in acknowledging any ways in which I have been disobedient to His Word, and how sorry I am for living in a way that does not glorify Him. I tell Him I am indeed sorry for things I've thought, said, or done that I know have broken His heart.

**T: Thanksgiving.** I have so much to be thankful for, and it is important that I practice gratitude for all God has done for me. Since I woke up this morning, I am grateful. I have food to eat, clothes on my back, and the shelter of a nice home. He has blessed me with a loving wife and daughter, with a meaningful vocational mission, and I am so thankful for that. Today is another opportunity to serve my family and those God puts in my path. Regular thanksgiving puts me in a humble and upbeat state of mind as I meditate on and thank God for the many blessings He has brought my way.

**S: Supplication.** After adoring the Lord for how great He is, confessing unconfessed sin to Him and appropriating His gracious forgiveness, and expressing heartfelt gratitude for all the blessings in my life, I am ready to take my needs before Him. I begin by praying that His Holy Spirit would guard my heart and guide me throughout the day. I pray for my wife and daughter. I pray for my staff. I ask God to keep His hand of blessing on our church. I pray through a list of requests that people have asked me to pray about. I intercede on behalf of those who are sick or have lost their jobs. I pray for those I know who are having trouble in their marriages. I ask the Lord to reveal Himself and work in the lives of those who know Him. I know He hears me when I speak to Him, and I am so honored to be able to go to Him in prayer.

Spending time with the Lord also reminds me of who I am to Him. The world has a way of labeling us. Do you believe you have been labeled "failure"? How about "addict"? You may feel like your label is "divorced." Or that you are labeled "bankrupt." Some of you may feel like you are labeled "fired" or "obese." There are so many labels. When we look in 1 Chronicles 4 we see a list of names of the descendants of Judah. Sometimes we like to skip over the genealogies, but when we do, we miss some treasures. In 1 Chronicles 4:9–10 the author pauses the list of names to tell us about an answered prayer from another "unlikely" person named Jabez.

> Jabez was more honorable than his brothers; and his mother called his name Jabez, saying, "Because I bore him in pain." Jabez called upon the God of Israel, saying, "Oh that you would bless me and

enlarge my border, and that your hand might be with me, and that you would keep me from harm so that it might not bring me pain!" And God granted what he asked.

Jabez was more honorable than his brothers, but his name meant "pain." That was his label: "pain." But see what the Bible tells us about how he overcame his label. He prayed. Prayer changes things, but more than anything, prayer changes you and me. Jabez may not have been from a family that believed in him, but he prayed to a God who did! Jabez prayed thirty-four words and the Lord answered him.

Friend, if you want to lead well, you need to begin your day before God. That time spent with the Lord can change you. Your past does not define you; your label does not define you. Let God alone label and define you by spending time with Him in prayer.

He will remind you that you are "fearfully and wonderfully made" (Psalm 139:14) and you are created in His image (Genesis 1:26). Time with Him helps us know we are deeply loved and that He holds every detail of our lives lovingly in His hands. Time with Him in prayer is time well spent.

**LET GOD ALONE LABEL AND DEFINE YOU.**

I have learned that my best work has often come out of my time invested in prayer. When I pray before a meeting, the meeting runs better. When I ask God to go before me as I walk into a store, I make better purchase decisions. When I ask Him to guard and guide my heart, I interact more lovingly with my family and my church staff. Prayer is essential to leading myself and others well. God has said to me, "Benny, you will never be more for Me in public than you are in private." If God is not doing something *in* you, He cannot do anything *through* you. How can God do something in you? You need to be alone with Him. Let Him speak to you, heal you, and hear you.

Where do I get this principle? The Bible. Let's look again at Nehemiah, cupbearer to King Artaxerxes in Persia, after he learned of the sad state of Jerusalem's wall and her people. Nehemiah 1:4 tells us, "As soon as I heard these words I sat down and wept and mourned for days, and I continued *fasting and praying* before the God of heaven" (emphasis added). Nehemiah was a man of prayer. He did not jump to action. He did not start offering advice on what he thought needed to be done. Nehemiah did not round up all his friends to get their opinions and thoughts. He fasted and prayed for four months before he told the king what was happening in Jerusalem. Nehemiah prayed and fasted.

The principle I want us to focus on here is that Nehemiah sought the Lord first. This is a great leadership principle that most leaders skip. Abraham Lincoln was a great example of a leader who prayed. He led our country during one of the most difficult times in United States history. He was recorded saying this during the Civil War: "I have been driven many times upon my knees by the overwhelming conviction that I had nowhere else to go. My own wisdom and that of all about me seemed insufficient for that day."[1] Leaders—especially Christian leaders—should go to God in prayer early and often!

In my experience prayer has been the single best thing I do every day. God is my best friend. He is the first person I speak to in the morning and the last person I converse with before I fall asleep at night. I ask God to go before me whether I'm entering time in His Word or entering a room. When I have a decision to make and don't know what to do, I seek God's counsel first by asking Him for wisdom and guidance.

I was reminded of the priority of prayer when I visited In Touch Ministries in Atlanta, which Dr. Charles Stanley led for so many years before going to heaven. My host asked if I would like to see Dr. Stanley's office, and as I stood in his office I noticed another, smaller room off to the side. "Tell me about that room," I asked. My host took me into the little room and told me it was Dr. Stanley's prayer room. That was where he would go to pray. On the floor was a mat where he would often kneel before the Lord. Dr. Stanley had always taught us young preachers to get on our knees and pray—an act of humbling ourselves before the Lord. Psalm 95:6 says, "Oh come, let us worship and bow down; let us kneel before the LORD, our Maker." I was so glad to be reminded of the necessity and power of prayer in a leader's life.

**WHEN I HAVE A DECISION TO MAKE, I SEEK GOD'S COUNSEL FIRST.**

There is another person in the Bible who gives us a powerful example of praying first: Jesus. At least twenty-five times in the Bible we are told that Jesus prayed. He prayed after He was baptized. He prayed when He was burdened. He prayed early in the morning, and He prayed all night. Most often He went away alone to pray.

Whenever I feel that I don't need to pray or that I'm too busy, all I have to do is look to Jesus to realize that if Jesus needed to pray on a regular basis, then I certainly need to pray!

One of my heroes in the faith, Dr. Charles Stanley (right)

There are people and situations that only you can pray for. You are the only person who will pray for your children with the passion and heart of their parent. You are the only person who will pray for your marriage and spouse the way you will. No one will pray for your grandchildren like you do. God wants to bless us. He wants to bless our families. When He blesses us, we can be a blessing to others. When we pray and ask God to bless us and we use our blessings to glorify Him, He can use that to increase our influence. Praying is the best way to care for yourself and those you lead.

Prayer is one of the most encouraging things we can do. When we let others know we are praying for them, it makes them feel seen and loved. When Paul wrote letters to the Philippian, Ephesian, and Colossian churches, he always let them know he was praying for them. I encourage you to let others know you are praying for them. There are times when you and I will get so discouraged in our lives that we cannot pray for ourselves. I've been there. Somebody saying "I'm praying for you, Benny" has meant the world to me. When my daughter, Savannah Abigail, was four or five years old and saw that I was going through a challenging time, she would say, "Daddy, I am going to pray for you." She would cup her little hands under my chin and pray for me. I would say to myself, "I know God is hearing that prayer!" It was so encouraging to me.

One of the most encouraging things for me right now happens when I come in on Sunday mornings and the first thing I see are men who will surround me and pray over me. It sets the tone of the day in our church, and others are blessed because those men took time to lift me up in prayer. Just as David had his "mighty men," I have my own group of "mighty men." When I need specific prayer, they are notified, and they pray for me. That makes all the difference in the world. I genuinely believe that the best way to lead others well is to make prayer the very first thing you do every day.

Yes, you can pray. We all need to pray, and it does not matter who you are or where you come from or how you feel labeled. You have immediate access to God in heaven through prayer, and He will help you with anything you face. There is nothing better you can do for your family. There is nothing more caring than praying for a friend or a coworker. If you want to be the best leader for everyone you encounter today, begin with prayer.

Yes, you need time alone with God!

## FOR REFLECTION

1. Are you satisfied with your prayer life? Why or why not?
2. What does your daily time with God look like? Why does this work for you?
3. What labels do you feel you have? How has God labeled you?
4. What do you think God is doing in your own life now?
5. Have you ever fasted before? What did you learn?
6. Do you regularly pray for others and let them know? How does that affect them—and you?

## PRINCIPLES TO REMEMBER

- Until God is doing something *in* you, He cannot do something *through* you.
- Daily time alone with God is the best way to be inwardly sound.
- When you don't know what to do, seek God's counsel first.
- If you don't know how to pray, remember the ACTS acrostic: adoration, confession, thanksgiving, supplication.
- Prayer changes things, but more than anything prayer changes you.
- Prayer is personal and when we pray, we can be blessed. When we are blessed, we can glorify God in the blessing. When God is glorified in the blessing, He has an opportunity to increase the blessing.

## CHAPTER 3
# YES, DISCIPLINE IS YOUR FRIEND

Every day I wake up between 4:45 a.m. and 5 a.m. I get out of bed, go to my car, and head to the gym. I take a run on a treadmill and come back home. I want to be honest with you; I was told that if I began exercising and continued for twenty-one days, I would start to enjoy it. That is a lie.

I do not wake up early every day and exercise because I enjoy it; I wake up early and exercise because I enjoy eating! Seriously, exercise has become a daily discipline for me because it gives me more energy and makes me better for my wife, family, staff, and church. Discipline is a gift that good leaders give themselves. Discipline is what it takes to get our inward leadership right; it sets us up to care for those we influence each day. A leader of a family, a leader of a small group, a leader among peers, a leader of children's church, and a leader of a business all have one thing in common—they stand out in a crowd because they know how to be alone without the crowd. They know how to be

> **DISCIPLINE IS THE BEHAVIOR YOU PRACTICE WHEN NO ONE ELSE IS LOOKING.**

alone because of discipline. Discipline is the behavior you practice when no one else is looking.

There are times when we overlook personal discipline because we think no one can see it. But people *can* see it. When self-discipline falters, the quality of our confidence and decision-making also falters. But when we know we have exercised discipline in any area of our lives, our self-confidence and thinking processes stabilize. Leaders lead better when they have confidence in themselves.

When it comes to caring for ourselves in order to lead others, knowing about your own self-discipline is important. Let me give you an example. There have been times when I have preached, and people will come up to me and tell me how good the sermon was. When they walked away, I would think, "If you only knew how the devil made me so busy this week that I could not spend the amount of time I needed to prepare my sermon." The devil cannot make me bad, but he can make me busy. Then I'd think, "What could that sermon have been if I would have had more time to study and prepare?"

For me, discipline is not just going to the gym. It is my daily time with God in prayer and in His Word. R. T. Kendall, the former pastor of Westminster Chapel in London, was a mentor to me for twenty-five years. One day I asked him what I needed to do to take my church to the next level. "You don't want to know," he replied. I asked him a couple more times, and his answer was the same. Finally, I pressed him, and he said, "OK. Two hours a day in prayer and Bible study to develop you."

*Yes, Discipline Is Your Friend*

R. T. Kendall (right) has been an incredible mentor in my life.

You see, for me to be my best for the church and for what God has called me to do, I need to make sure that I am in God's Word and praying every day. You do not have much to share if your cup is not running over. I might be able to preach a time or two without spending the amount of time necessary to do God's will in my life, but I can tell when I've fallen short in my time with God and His Word. Others notice too.

If you are a parent, you may need to embrace the discipline of rising a bit earlier in the morning to study the Bible and talk with God. If you are a student, you may need to develop the discipline to study each subject a little more each day. If you want to begin hiking, you will need to begin walking in an area with some hills. Determine the area of your life that needs more time and develop a new discipline to help you grow in that area. Discipline is not about liking the process; it is about becoming the best version of yourself for those you lead.

Another discipline leaders should consider growing is the art of hearing from the Lord. Elijah, a prophet of the Lord during the reign of King Ahab, was disciplined in hearing God speak to him and doing what God told him to do. In 1 Kings 17:3, the Lord told Elijah, "Hide yourself by the brook Cherith." In chapter 18 God told him, "Go, show yourself," so Elijah obeyed. When God told Elijah to go, Elijah went. When God told Elijah to stay, he stayed. We should spend time in prayer every day, but we should also take the time to listen and hear from God. To care for others at my absolute best and for God to be able to do extraordinary things in my life, I must be disciplined to do what God has called me to do.

Nehemiah shows us that daily discipline matters. In Nehemiah 1 we see that Nehemiah heard about the wall in the "month of Chislev, in the twentieth year." Nehemiah 2 then tells us, "And it came about in the month Nisan, in the twentieth year..." (NASB). On our calendars the Hebrew month of Chislev runs from mid-November to mid-December; Nisan is mid-March to mid-April. So from the time Nehemiah learned about the sad state of Jerusalem to when he could speak with King Artaxerxes about it, four months had passed. What did Nehemiah do between those moments? He was disciplined enough to pray and fast and wait until the Lord provided him with the right opportunity.

As leaders, we must exercise discipline in every area of our lives. Discipline is not just about working out and reading our Bibles. Discipline is not just what we do to teach our children the lessons of life. Nehemiah shows us that discipline is also waiting on God for the right timing. There are many times when we think we know what is best, and we ask God for things and do not give Him the time He needs to answer. We don't know all the challenges Nehemiah faced in those four months, but God used that time to prepare him for the bigger job. God used His timing to build Nehemiah's faith to do something extraordinary: rebuild the wall of Jerusalem.

When we are not disciplined to wait on God, we may not have the faith to get through certain situations. Our character may not be sufficiently prepared to handle the pressure that comes with a decision we've hastened to make on our own. Taking the time to wait on God for His guidance can save us from hurting ourselves and those we lead. For those of us who feel "unlikely," discipline is one of the things God uses to enable us to accomplish something extraordinary for Him.

Abraham Lincoln said, "Discipline is choosing between what you want now and what you want most."[1] If you want more energy, you need the discipline to expend energy. So you exercise when you feel like you don't have the energy to exercise. You don't wait to "feel" energy or until you have time on the calendar. You use this as an opportunity to do the uncomfortable. If you want to grow your mind, you need to read more books. You don't wait until you feel like reading; you pick a book in an area in which you'd like to grow and read every day. You *make* it happen. One page at a time, every day. If you want to grow spiritually, you carve out and reserve the time to study Scripture and pray daily. You can set your alarm earlier or stay up a bit later. If your children tend to wake up while you are having your quiet time, invite them in. (Your children are not a distraction; they are a divine appointment!) A little bit of time with them pays huge dividends.

Improving your inward leadership is not a list of enjoyable things to do. It is doing what no one else is willing to do so you can care for those no one else can care for. This is what I have learned about life. It is trial by the mile. It is hard by the yard. But it is a cinch by the inch. To be an extraordinary leader, you must prepare yourself. To start being disciplined in any area of your life, start small—but start. Then, as you realize the benefits of self-discipline, gradually take on additional areas of growth as the Lord leads you.

**TO START BEING DISCIPLINED IN ANY AREA OF YOUR LIFE, START SMALL— BUT START.**

If you are thinking about how to be the best leader for your life circumstance, your family, your workplace, or your relationships, start with doing something little today that is different from yesterday. For me, it is a matter of beginning with something small, applying the small amount of time, energy, and effort daily over time, and watching it grow into something only God can do. If this works for me, I know it can work for you too!

Yes, you can be disciplined in your life!

## FOR REFLECTION

1. In what areas of your life do you feel you have discipline? What areas of your life do you think lack discipline?

2. Just as the Lord told Elijah to "hide himself" and "show himself," He will do the same for you. Which of these seasons do you believe you are in?

3. Discipline can also mean waiting on the Lord. Has there been a time when you had to wait on the Lord? What happened?

4. How does discipline start? What do your feelings have to do with that?

5. What is something small that you can do today to start cultivating discipline?

## PRINCIPLES TO REMEMBER

- Discipline is a gift that good leaders give to themselves.
- Discipline is the behavior you practice when no one else is looking.
- Daily disciplines develop character and personal growth.
- Discipline begins with something small, applying daily time and effort that eventually grows into something only God can do in and through you.

## CHAPTER 4

# YES, YOU WERE CREATED ON PURPOSE FOR A PURPOSE

THE THREE GREATEST days of your life are the day you were born, the day you were born again, and the day you realize why you were born. Finding your purpose is exceedingly difficult for many people, and perhaps for you. Why? You may have multiple gifts. You may be gifted in music and technology; you may be creative and have a speaking ability. You may be gifted in business and mechanics. I will tell you, finding my purpose was not difficult for me. I am not a super-gifted person. It was easier for me to learn God's purpose for my life because I did not have multiple abilities. My purpose is simple: to pastor Rock Springs Church effectively, and to help other pastors lead their churches. It is that simple for me.

Which is why I don't go on three mission trips a year. Mission trips are not God's purpose for my life. Mission trips may be God's purpose for your life, but I know they aren't His purpose for my life. I know what my purpose is, and I know why I was born. I am passionate about what God has called me to do, which helps me remember my purpose. Whether it is Mother Teresa serving the less fortunate in Calcutta or Winston Churchill standing against the tyranny of Hitler, they knew their purpose. They were passionate about their cause, and they influenced many people with their purpose and passion.

My early days as a preacher

Effective leaders have a powerful sense of purpose that is driven by passion.

I know many successful leaders who did not have passion behind their purpose. Where do I get this idea? Jesus. In John 9:4 Jesus tells His disciples, "We must work the works of him who sent me while it is day; night is coming, when no one can work." Notice that Jesus said, "We *must*." There was another time when Jesus was young, and His parents had lost Him on their way home from Jerusalem. When they finally found Him in the temple, Mary asked, "Son, why have you treated us so? Behold, your father and I have been searching for you in great distress." Twelve-year-old Jesus replied, "Why were you looking for me? Did you not know that *I must be in my Father's house*?" (Luke 2:48–49, emphasis added).

I firmly believe that if you take care of God's business, He will take care of your business. Jesus was passionate about His purpose. In your life, there will be things that are not just opportunities, they are opportunities you *must* do. You'll feel it like a fire in your bones. My reason for existence is that I must preach the gospel. That is my purpose, and it is driven by my passion. When you tap into your passion, you will not need the alarm clock very much because your passion will wake you up every morning. When you find your passion, you'll know your purpose. Passion produces energy. Passion produces excellence. Passion is what produces endurance. Passion communicates your purpose.

God has given each of us a purpose, and when we are walking in our purpose, we stand out among our peers. Paul encourages us in 1 Corinthians 15:58, "Therefore, my beloved brothers, be steadfast, immovable, always abounding in the *work of the Lord*, knowing that in the Lord your labor is not in vain" (emphasis added). The source of our passion and purpose is God. When you are working with passion inside your purpose, nothing you do will be in vain. The source of your passion is what God has done, what God is doing, and what God is going to do in and through you!

God has gifted you with your purpose. When you are leading within God's will for your life, you'll feel His pleasure.

I believe when you think of an effective leader, you can almost immediately think of one word to define their purpose. Defined purpose is easily described. It does not take ten words to describe them.

Did Nehemiah have a powerful sense of purpose? In Nehemiah 2, when King Artaxerxes asked Nehemiah why he was downcast, Nehemiah breathed a quick prayer and told him the problem: "The city, the place of my fathers' graves, lies in ruins, and its gates have been destroyed by fire" (v. 3). The king asked Nehemiah what he was requesting. After praying to God again, he responded, "Send me to Judah, to the city of my fathers' graves, that I may rebuild it" (v. 5). With a powerful sense of purpose, Nehemiah was able to lay out a clear plan to the king, tell him the resources needed to make the journey to Judah successful, name the authorizations needed to travel without interference, and cite the resources and people he needed to make the trip. Nehemiah's sense of purpose gave him clear direction.

**DEFINED PURPOSE IS EASILY DESCRIBED.**

Most people with a powerful sense of purpose do not have a tough time convincing others to join them in their passions because they are able to state their purpose so clearly. They are also using their God-given gifts to organize and achieve the vision God has given them. This does not mean that the roads are easy; it just means that when you have a passion and a purpose, the drive outweighs the challenges.

So how do you discover your purpose? First, you pray. I know this sounds like a broken record, but you have a direct line to the God who created you in His image. As the apostle Paul reminds us, "For we are his workmanship, created in Christ Jesus for good works, which God prepared beforehand, that we should walk in them" (Ephesians 2:10). Why would you not lean into the One who designed you to show you what you were created to do? He has good plans for you, and He invites you to invite Him into your life and leadership. When you're doing what you were created to do, you never have to work another day in your life. A job is what you get paid for; a calling (purpose) is what you were made for. And when you know what you were made for, it is a fun journey—with Jesus and the Holy Spirit guiding your steps.

The next thing to do is find what comes naturally to you and begin doing that. What do you do in your daily life that others think is difficult but to you is not a big deal? If you find that an activity, habit, or task comes naturally to you, you may have found your purpose. Spend time asking God what your purpose is and how He would like for you to develop your gift for His glory. He will open and close doors to direct you.

**A JOB IS WHAT YOU GET PAID FOR; PURPOSE IS WHAT YOU WERE MADE FOR.**

You may be in a season that has you thinking you were made for more than what you are doing in this moment. You might be a single parent who finds it hard to make it to the next paycheck. You may be in a season of bad decisions, and you cannot seem to find a way out of the mess you are in. You might be a student who does not feel old enough to make big decisions. You could be an employee in a large corporation who feels you are not being used to your fullest potential. You may have made terrible mistakes from which you feel there is no recovery.

Friend, you were created on purpose for a purpose and

the God of all creation has a plan for your life no matter where you are right now. If He makes clear the purpose of your life and it is not where you are right now, trust Him to open the next door or create a way out of your situation.

Developing your purpose may mean sacrificing some things. You may lose some sleep so you can go back to school to get the education and skills you need. You may need to defer a purchase you've saved for in order to move your purpose forward. You may need to sacrifice some time with friends so you can pursue what God has called you to. Whatever the sacrifice is, it is worth it! There is freedom in finding what God created you to do, and you will experience the peace and joy of knowing you are in the middle of His will.

Not only has He created you with specific gifts and talents, He has also given you your life experience that makes you the perfect person for a specific task. He may place a burden on your heart to intercede for others in prayer. You may love hosting people in your home, which ministers acceptance and friendship. God may have given you a detail-oriented mindset to help big-picture colleagues complete projects with excellence. God gives some of His people the gift of discernment to help those in the church correct spiritual missteps and get back in line with God's plan for them. Some Christians have the gift of giving; they are especially adept at making and giving money so the church can continue its ministry and outreach. The list goes on and on.

Some mistakenly think that what they are doing cannot be their purpose because it is not inside the walls of a church. But Jesus needs people outside the church walls to be His representatives who invite others in for a safe place to heal and grow. Our purpose is not dependent on working inside a church or in a high-paying job. Our purpose is to use our giftings where God has planted us to draw others to Him for His glory!

God is a God of infinitely more! He will take your circumstance, your job, your family, your mistakes, your heartbreaks, and disappointments and turn them around for His glory. God definitely has a purpose for you—and yes, you can lead yourself to discover your passion and your purpose.

**LEADING YOURSELF FIRST MEANS GETTING RIGHT WITH YOU.**

If you've struggled to find out what God created you to do, several spiritual gifts tests are available that can help. See the appendix for a test that can reveal what you're seeking. (You won't even have to study for it!)

Leading yourself first means getting right with you. I have learned that if I am not right with the Lord and don't first have myself in order, then I cannot bring my best to those I lead. And since I care so deeply for those God has entrusted to my care, I need to make sure I'm right with God every morning and throughout the day. With the Holy Spirit's guidance and strength, I'm able to continually focus on my passion and purpose so I can best fulfill God's will for my life: loving and caring for those He has brought into my sphere of influence.

And if I can do it, then yes, you can!

## FOR REFLECTION

1. Do you remember the day you were born again? How has that impacted your life?
2. Do you feel you have a sense of purpose in your life? If so, what is it?
3. If you do not feel a sense of purpose in your life, what is something you often do that you enjoy and that comes easily to you?
4. What do you dream about? What would you do if you could do whatever you wanted to do?
5. What do you weep about? For many, their passion and purpose come out of pain.
6. What are your spiritual gifts? Do you utilize them? In what ways? How could you better use those gifts for God's kingdom?
7. How will you continue to develop your purpose to help others around you?

## PRINCIPLES TO REMEMBER

- The source of your purpose is God.
- Effective leaders can often be described in one or two words that define their purpose.
- Leaders with a defined purpose don't often have a hard time getting out of bed in the morning.
- When you find what you are passionate about, your purpose becomes clear.

- Purpose often comes from God's direction, and the specific gifts and talents He has given you will help you define your purpose more clearly.

# PART II

# LEADING THOSE WHO WALK BESIDE YOU

*People don't care how much you know until they know how much you care.*
—**Author Unknown**

CHAPTER 5

# YES, LEADERSHIP IS SERVING OTHERS

IN THE NEXT few chapters we'll focus on leading those who walk beside you, people like your spouse, a coworker, and a friend. When we remember that leading is not just something we do in the workplace, it enables us to view every relationship as an opportunity to influence and care.

I do not see myself as better than anyone. Leading is not about being better; it is about influence and care. The best way to influence and care for others is to serve them. On occasion, people have asked me how they can lead people who are on the same level or in the same position. How do I lead my spouse? How do I lead my friends or peers? Here's how: Make sure your life is about serving. When you are with your family, or you are at work, or you are with your friends, look for ways to serve those around you.

**EVERY RELATIONSHIP IS AN OPPORTUNITY TO CARE.**

If serving is beneath you, then leadership will always be above you. Albert Schweitzer put it this way: "I don't know what your destiny will be, but one thing I know: The only ones among you who will be really happy are those who will have sought and found how to serve."[1]

How will you know the best way to serve those around you? Listen to them. If you lean in and pay attention, they'll reveal their deepest need, and you can serve them there. Listen to those around you as they speak to others. Listen when they are communicating with you. Some people need time. Others may need quiet. Some people need rest. There may be someone who needs you to take their children for an hour. Listen empathetically to discover where you can meet a need. If you learn to do that, you will be leading and caring for those around you by serving humbly. And humble service can make a huge difference.

You lead best by serving.

When I think about servant leadership, I think of Jesus and His disciples in the upper room at Passover. Jesus knew He was about to begin His journey to the cross. Jesus and His disciples were having their Passover meal, what has become known as the Last Supper. I can imagine there being a basin and a towel in the room. John 13:4–5 tells us that Jesus "rose from supper. He laid aside his outer garments, and taking a towel, tied it around his waist. Then he poured water into a basin and began to wash the disciples' feet and to wipe them with the towel that was wrapped around him."

Jesus was the only one who picked up a towel and washed the feet of the disciples. The twelve guys who had entered the room with Jesus had walked past the basin and the towel. Jesus led by serving. In John 13:15, Jesus tells His disciples, "For I have given you an example, that you also should do just as I have done to you." This is the only time Jesus said that He has given an example, and the example was that He washed the feet of His disciples.

The reason for the basin and towels was that most people

walked at this time in history. Their shoes, if they had them, were more like sandals. The roads they walked were the same roads on which animals transported people. So the roads were ripe with animal waste and dirt. The basin and towels were in the room, ready to be used, but not one of the disciples thought to serve by washing the feet of their colleagues. Jesus gave them (and us) a real-life example of how to care for people: Humble yourself and meet a need. Serve.

Jesus, their leader, was not into titles. He was into towels.

As I read that account, the Lord said to me, "Benny, how many times have you walked past the basin and towels?" There are basins and towels in every relationship. There are basins and towels in every workplace. There are basins and towels in every ministry. What are your basins? What are your towels?

**JESUS WAS NOT INTO TITLES. HE WAS INTO TOWELS.**

I'm embarrassed to admit that there are times when I walk right past the towels and look to see how others can serve me. How about you? You and I need to take off the bib we wear that says, "Serve Me" and wrap ourselves in a towel to serve others. Instead of waiting for somebody to do something for you, look for a meaningful way help somebody else.

Here's another helpful way to examine yourself: "Am I a window person or a mirror person?" If you are a window person, you usually look out to see who you can serve. If you are a mirror person, you typically look at yourself and wonder who can serve you. When our core identity is in Jesus Christ, we become more aware of how and where we can serve others. As Howard G. Hendricks said, "There was no identity crisis in the life of Jesus Christ. He knew who He was. He knew where He had come from and why He was here. And He knew where He was going. And when you are that liberated, then you can serve."[2] When we get our eyes off ourselves and look to Jesus, we are in a much better position to serve others. Those who serve others lead well.

Serving often means being willing—even eager—to do something that other people have walked right past or are not willing to do. In our homes it could be taking out the trash without being asked, putting dishes in the dishwasher for the family, cutting the grass when others have been busy, or taking on another household chore that someone hasn't gotten to. We should be more like Christ at home than anywhere! If it is with family and friends, it may mean being gentle and kind, listening, or even keeping our mouths shut. In the workplace, serving may look like picking up trash that has fallen to the ground and others have ignored, noticing if someone needs help on a task, and jumping to assist without anyone else knowing.

Serving others might even involve helping those who may not really deserve help, as well as those who are enemies. Jesus reminds us, "You have heard that it was said, 'You shall love your neighbor and hate your enemy.' But I say to you, Love your enemies and pray for those who persecute you, so that you may be sons of your Father who is in heaven" (Matthew 5:43–45). And the apostle Paul backs this up in 1 Corinthians 9:19: "For though I am free from all, I have made myself a servant to all, that I might win more of them."

We're not saved to sit. We are saved to serve.

Leading those with whom we live and work often means taking our eyes off ourselves and seeing another's

*Yes, Leadership Is Serving Others*

needs. Putting others first does not mean losing our position with them or ceasing to be who we are. Putting others first is leading by caring, just as Jesus did.

Another way to serve others is to go the extra mile. You may say, "Benny, where did you get this?" The Bible! Jesus taught us so much about how to lead. In Matthew 5:41 He addressed the principle of the extra mile: "And if anyone forces you to go one mile, go with him two miles."

When Jesus taught this principle, the Jewish people were under Roman authority. If a Roman soldier was walking a road and came across a Jewish person, he could force that person to carry his backpack, shield, or sword one mile, and the Jew had no choice; it was Roman law. The Jewish people knew that it was 5,280 feet to reach a mile, and they taught their children how to count each step. Once the Jewish person got to the mile marker, they could drop the Roman soldier's items and get back to what they were doing. What Jesus was teaching here was to take the Roman soldier's personal things and carry them not one but two miles! Jesus knew that the first mile was the duty-filled mile. He knew the second mile was the difference-making mile.

The extra-mile principle can revolutionize your leadership. Ecclesiastes 9:10 tells us, "Whatever your hand finds to do, do it with all your might." Paul writes in Colossians 3:23, "Whatever you do, work heartily, as for the Lord and not for men." When you do it with a smile and style, with no reluctance, then you are going the extra mile.

Vocation comes from the Latin word *vocare*, and it means "a calling." If you are a nurse, you are called. If you are an attorney, you are called. If you are a fireman, you are called. If you are a teacher, you are called. If you are a businessman, you are called. If you are in law enforcement, you are called. Whatever your vocation, you are called. God wants us to go the extra mile in our work because it sets us apart from others. What if we got to work early and left late? What would that tell our boss? When you are willing to do more than you are required to do in your work, there is a blessing that comes from going the extra mile.

Here is a beautiful example of leadership with a heart to serve by going the extra mile. We were having a men's breakfast at our church, and we had asked the CEO of a company to come and speak. It was getting close to time for the program to begin and the speaker was not there. I was beginning to think I needed to come up with something fast. I looked around the room and I saw someone who was not on our staff serving coffee and cleaning tables. As I watched more closely, I realized he was our speaker. He had just come in, rolled up his sleeves, and started serving coffee, chatting with the men, and bussing tables! What a down-to-earth example of servant leadership!

Jesus is not the only biblical example of serving those around us. In Nehemiah 2:10 we read that as Nehemiah was on his way to Jerusalem, he came across a Samaritan leader and an Ammonite official who were very displeased that "someone had come to seek the welfare of the people of Israel." Notice, Nehemiah did not go back to his homeland for himself. He went to Jerusalem seeking the welfare of the children of Israel. Nehemiah was heading back to care for and serve the people who were there. As we see with Nehemiah, serving others is not always received well. Serving others is also not what most people would consider "leadership." But as I look at leadership in the Bible, here is what I have found. The word *leader* is used

*Yes, Leadership Is Serving Others*

fewer than ten times. The word *servant* is used more than a thousand times. This tells me that God's heart is more about us serving others. If God thinks it important that we humble ourselves and serve others, then I should make it a practice in my leadership.

This reminds me of a time Horst Schulze came to speak to our staff. I will never forget one of the things he said in that meeting: "We are just ladies and gentlemen serving ladies and gentlemen."

I've spent time learning excellence from Horst Shulze (left).

When leading, always be looking for ways to serve. Serve in your workplace, serve in your church, and serve in your family. Willingly, graciously. Saved people should serve people.

Yes, you can lead by serving others!

## FOR REFLECTION

1. Why is serving as a leader important?

2. Leadership is not always about the one talking. As a leader, do you take time to truly listen to those you serve? What would change about your leadership if you listened more?

3. Jesus gave us a great example of serving those He was leading. How can you better serve those around you?

4. What are some opportunities to serve that you might tend to walk right by? How could you begin taking action to serve others in those ways?

5. How can you go the extra mile with those you spend time with every day? What can you do to go the extra mile at home and at work?

6. How does being aware that your job is your "calling" inspire you to lead differently at work?

## PRINCIPLES TO REMEMBER

- The best way to influence others is to serve them.

- The best way to serve others is by being attentive and listening to them.

- As a leader, Jesus was not into titles; He was into towels. We should seek to look for basins and towels in our leadership.

- Serving others is being willing to do what others are not willing to do.

- Serving others is going the extra mile.

CHAPTER 6

# YES, YOU CAN ENCOURAGE OTHERS

I WAS HONORED TO visit Truett Cathy, founder of Chick-fil-A, in his home before he passed away. He said to me, "Benny, do you know how to tell if a person needs encouragement?"

Well, I was thinking that something profound was coming from a man like this, so I leaned in and said, "Mr. Cathy, please tell me how to know."

Truett said, "If they are breathing."

What truth and wisdom in that simple statement! I can tell you that everyone you will encounter every day wears an invisible necklace that reads, "Help me feel good about myself." Everyone needs encouragement. Encouragement can make someone smile when they are going through a rough time. Encouragement can make people who are down on themselves feel better about themselves. Encouragement can help those around you stay motivated when things get hard. It is a documented fact that if you are barefoot and made to stand in ice water, you can stand in it twice as long if someone is there to encourage you.

Because I know too well the sadness a child experiences from lack of encouragement, I made special effort to encourage my daughter as she grew up. All her life I told her, "Yes, you can!" Whatever she said she wanted to do, I made sure to tell her she was capable. Nearly every day I would ask her, "What is the smartest and prettiest girl in the world doing today?" We need to believe in people and encourage them until they can believe in themselves—especially those inside our homes. If we are going to influence those around us, we need to remember that *everyone* needs encouragement—and when they receive it, they'll enjoy a far more fulfilling and productive life.

Saul, who was hunting people who followed Jesus when we first met him in the Book of Acts, became one of the greatest unlikely leaders in the Bible. He met Jesus one day, his life was transformed, he was given a new name (Paul), and he ended up writing the majority of the New Testament letters. Once he began spreading the gospel, Paul often found himself in prison. When he was imprisoned in Rome, someone he had led to the Lord, Onesiphorus, would seek him out and visit him. Paul said of Onesiphorus that "he often refreshed me" or "he often encouraged me" (2 Timothy 1:16). If the great apostle needed encouragement, and it meant enough to him to mention it in his letter to Timothy, I believe everyone we are around needs encouragement too!

**IF YOU WANT TO BE A LEADER WHO TRULY CARES FOR THOSE AROUND YOU, ENCOURAGE THEM WITH YOUR WORDS.**

If you want to be a leader who truly cares for those around you, encourage them with your words. Let me share real-life examples from my life.

I remember playing recreational baseball in sixth grade. I was not the best player on my team, and I was definitely the smallest! There was a coach who everyone wanted to play for. Anyone playing baseball in my town wanted this coach to pick them for his team. Well, this highly sought-after coach didn't pick me.

One day my team faced this coach's team. I was playing third base, and his team was at bat. One of his players hit a grounder at me and I scooped it up and I threw the runner out. I will never forget what happened next. That highly esteemed coach came up to me and quietly said, "Good play, little man." Here I am, sixty years old now, and I have never forgotten those words. Encouraging words matter.

In Genesis 1:3 we see that "God said..." How did this beautiful world come into existence? God spoke it into existence. Words created this world, and words can create people's worlds. Proverbs 18:21 tells us, "Death and life are in the power of the tongue." Paul wrote, "Let no unwholesome word come your mouth, but if there is any good word for edification according to the need of the moment, say that, so that it will give grace to those who hear" (Ephesians 4:29, NASB). Hebrews 3:13 says, "But exhort [encourage] one another every day."

Since the Scriptures instruct us to encourage and exhort one another daily, we disobey God if we are not encouraging those around us. And for many, this takes practice. We need to be looking for things to praise instead of criticize. Marriages, homes, businesses, and churches are healthier environments when encouragement is among their core values. Imagine what your marriage would look like if you spoke encouragement instead of criticism. How would your children act if you look for positive things on which to commend them instead of correcting everything they do? What would work look like if everyone would stop complaining about the workplace and begin highlighting what's right? I believe we will be better positioned to lead and influence others when we offer sincere, encouraging words.

One day in a staff meeting I handed each person a blank sheet of paper. I asked them all to write three positive things about the person on their right. I asked them not to sign their comments but to turn them in to me. Then I began reading them aloud. I read words and phrases such as *thoughtful, polite, willing to go the extra mile*, and my staff started naming those they felt the words represented. After hearing the encouraging words my team started saying things like "I didn't know you felt that way about me" or "I didn't know you saw that in me." Our work environment became a more positive place. You can do this in any environment: work, home, or a gathering of friends. Those in your company and care will all be uplifted. Everyone works harder when they are encouraged!

**EVERYONE WORKS HARDER WHEN THEY ARE ENCOURAGED!**

One of the most moving moments of my life came at my eighth-grade graduation. Earlier that year the principal at my school, Phyllis Lusk, had been driving home behind a school bus. She saw the bus stop at a house where, she had learned, whiskey was sold illegally. She watched as one of her students was dropped off there. That student was me.

So my principal knew where I lived. She knew what kind of life I lived. She knew that I helped Mama sell alcohol from our house. Phyllis Lusk knew I did not make good grades. But I will never forget part of her address to the eighth grade at our graduation. She said, "I see a doctor, I see a nurse, I see a teacher, I see a businessman."

*Yes, You Can Encourage Others*

And if I live to be a hundred, I will never forget what she said next: "I see a preacher."

In that moment, I felt a voice in my heart say, "It's you." Phyllis knew where I came from. She must have thought I would not make much of myself. But at that graduation, her encouraging words gave me hope. All these years later, if I am ever preaching near her home, she comes to see me.

Here I am with my eighth-grade teacher, Phyllis Lusk.

I must share one more story of how encouragement literally changed my life.

My stepfather always spoke unkindly to me. He was

often critical of what I said or did or failed to do. He never hesitated to tell me I was ignorant and that I wouldn't amount to anything. And I've already mentioned that I didn't do very well in school.

One day my mama loaded me, my sister, my stepbrother, and my stepsister in the car and said we were all going to the doctor for physicals. Later, though, I learned that I would not be getting a physical like my siblings but would get a mental evaluation because I could not learn, comprehend, or retain information. I am here to tell you that it's true: "Death and life are in the power of the tongue." When you are told almost every day that you are ignorant, you believe it. When you believe negative words spoken about you, you become what you are told. I struggled mightily through my teen years, early adulthood, and even early in my Christian walk, to overcome all the cruel words I had been subjected to.

But wait, there's more.

My mama divorced my stepfather. I gave my life to Jesus Christ. Mama started dating a man named Don Mason. Then, as I grew into a young man, I felt the call to preach, and Don came to hear me. He asked what I was going to do with my life. I told him I worked as a janitor and cleaned commodes for $3.35 per hour. Don said, "Well, you are a preacher."

I told him, "I am preaching on street corners. I am preaching in jails. I am preaching at a rescue mission. I am preaching wherever I can, but I have to clean commodes to make a living." Don replied, "No, you can be so much more than that. You need to go to Bible college." I reminded Don that I had failed in school, and I'd never make it in college. And Don said, "Yes, you can! You are smart." I had never, ever had a man tell me I was smart. Before I met Don, there had been only one other man in my life, and he had told me over and over that I was dumb.

Don went on to offer, "Every degree you complete, I will pay for." I went on to complete my associate's, bachelor's, master's, and doctorate! Don paid for all of them.

I am not saying this to boast on anyone other than God, but in those Bible classes I never made anything other than A's. I had one guy who didn't believe in me as a child, and I failed in school. I had another guy who did believe in me, and I made straight A's. Tell me there is no power in encouraging people. The way you see people is the way you treat people. The way you treat people is often the way they become. Encouraging words matter!

So how can you provide an encouraging environment in your home, your workplace, your circle of friends? Here is one group exercise I've found helpful.

On a white board, I draw a line down the middle. At the top left I write *Skills* and at the top right I write *Attributes*. I pick one person in the group and ask them to pick a person who has been an encouragement to them. Then I have the "picker" name the things their chosen person does to encourage others, and I write these down. If it is a skill, it goes on the left side of the board. If it is an attribute, I list it on the right side of the line. Now watch this: Ninety-nine percent of the time, the person I selected cites *attributes* of the person they're commending.

I then point out to the group that attributes are what matter, and we need to encourage people with positive, affirming words about their attributes. Not all of us have all the skills, but we all have attributes or character traits worthy of praise. If you are a parent with young children, remember that encouragement means everything to them. This doesn't mean you spoil them or fail to discipline them when necessary. Raising emotionally healthy children means bringing them up in the fear and admonition of the Lord, balanced by a generous lifestyle of hearty, loving, caring encouragement along the way. If you are a teacher or children's Sunday school leader, your encouraging words can make a lasting impact on the children in your care. If you are married, encouraging and affirming words can change the dynamics of your relationship for a more positive experience. If you are at work with people and your boss is always telling all of you what you're doing wrong or what can be done better, your kind words can change the attitude of your department. You don't need to be a boss to influence the direction of the people you work with.

Another way to encourage others is to be a peacemaker and practice forgiveness. Jesus said in Matthew 5:9, "Blessed are the peacemakers, for they will be called sons of God." I have lived long enough to learn that the greatest blessings in our lives are tied to forgiveness. It is amazing what God wants to do in our lives, but it will always involve forgiving other people. Consider a letter the apostle Paul wrote to Philemon from a Roman prison. Paul was a great encourager. Philemon is the only letter in the Bible written to a layman, and it's only twenty-five verses long.

Here's the back story: Philemon had a slave named Onesimus who had stolen from him, escaped, and traveled thirteen hundred miles to Rome. When he got to Rome, Paul led him to faith in Christ. So Paul wrote to Philemon on behalf of the repentant slave. Paul acknowledged what

Onesimus had done, then went on to write, "But if he has wronged you in any way or owes you anything, charge that to my account" (Philemon 18, NASB). Paul was asking Philemon to forgive Onesimus for his own sake. When we forgive, everybody wins.

As a leader, you want your team to win. When you forgive, everybody wins. Harboring unforgiveness is like drinking poison and expecting the other person to die. When we don't forgive people, it destroys us. Bitterness does more damage to the container in which it is stored than to the object on which it is poured. When we don't forgive, we hurt ourselves as well as those we lead. Forgiveness encourages the giver, the receiver, and those around them.

Ephesians 4:32 tells us, "Be kind to one another, tenderhearted, forgiving one other, as God in Christ forgave you." We need to remember that we have all sinned and offended others. As leaders, we need to be an example to our family, our peers, our friends, and our neighbors by extending forgiveness. If you are in a place where you are not sure if you have fully forgiven someone, here is a test: Try to pray a blessing over them. If you cannot do that, you may not have fully forgiven them yet. Jesus told us that we are blessed if we are peacemakers. When we remember what He did for us as our leader, we should do the same for others. We should be peacemakers—kind, tenderhearted, and forgiving, just as God in Christ has forgiven us.

**WHEN WE FORGIVE, EVERYBODY WINS.**

Another benefit of encouraging others is that it often comes back to encourage us as well. I have often told the story of how, years ago, a man named Clayton Jones got up at midnight to come to our home, where we were selling whiskey illegally, so he could lead a lost sixteen-year-old boy to new life in Jesus Christ. Nearly every Sunday since, as I get in my car to head to church to preach, I pick up my phone and dial Clayton's number. When he answers, I thank him for that one act of encouragement in the middle of the night so many years ago. And Clayton always replies, "I started out as your pastor, now you pastor me." Encouragement has come full circle.

Maya Angelou once said, "I've learned that people will forget what you said, people will forget what you did, but people will never forget how you made them feel."[1]

How do *you* make people feel?

## FOR REFLECTION

1. Have you ever been encouraged by someone's words? What were those words? How did they make you feel?

2. Proverbs 18:21 says, "Death and life is in the power of the tongue." Have you found this to be true in your own interactions?

3. How would encouraging others help you be a good leader to them?

4. How would encouragement in the form of forgiveness help you as a leader?

5. Has someone ever inspired you to become better by their words? Who was that person? How did you feel?

6. Contemplate: How do *you* make people feel?

## PRINCIPLES TO REMEMBER

- God's words created this world, and our words can create people's worlds.

- Everyone works harder when they are encouraged.

- We can encourage others with our words by speaking words of affirmation, words of praise, words that inspire, and words from the Bible.

- We can also encourage others by being an example of peacemaking and forgiveness.

- Encouragement often comes full circle.

## CHAPTER 7

# YES, YOU SHOULD PREFER OTHERS

Here is part of a song by Charles D. Meigs that I try to read aloud every day:

> Lord, help me live from day to day
> In such a self-forgetful way,
> That even when I kneel to pray
> My prayer should be for others.
> Yes, others, Lord, yes others,
> Let this my motto be...
> Help me live for others,
> That I may live like Thee.[1]

When leading people in my sphere of influence, I often need to remind myself that life is not about me—it is about serving others, actually regarding them as more important than myself. Philippians 2:3 instructs, "Do nothing from selfish ambition or conceit, but *in humility count others more significant than yourselves*" (emphasis added). Good leaders make every effort to "prefer" the people around them over themselves by considering their needs, desires, challenges, and viewpoints as "more significant" than their own. There's an old, trustworthy acronym that helps us remember this biblical principle: JOY—Jesus, Others, Yourself.

Live and lead by this sequence and you'll live and lead with JOY, demonstrating to those you influence that you truly care about them. So as I talk with God at the start of my day, I make a point to consider the intentional things I can do for those He puts in my path. Who can I bless with Barbara's banana bread? How can I show sincere interest in the people I come across? Who do I want to especially encourage? Who needs to hear me say I believe in them? When someone on our staff accomplishes a milestone in life, how will I tell them how proud I am of them? I want to thank people who do things for me. I want to write cards to those who are celebrating birthdays or anniversaries. These are simple, uncomplicated ways to think of others more than myself, but what a difference they can make to those in my care. As Mary Kay Ash said, "Everyone has an invisible sign around their neck that says, 'Make me feel important.' Never forget this message when working with people."[2]

**PREFERRING OTHERS OVER YOURSELF IS A CHOICE.**

How do you "count others more significant than [yourself]"? Preferring others over yourself is a choice, and you can ask God each day to help you see others first.

If I can find it within myself to let others know I'm proud of them or that they have priority over me, they may not struggle with self-esteem or wonder where they stand with me. Sometimes preferring another is simply saying, "I'm proud of you." Scripture even tells us that God did this for Jesus. Think of it: Jesus had just begun His ministry. He had not performed His first miracle. He had not walked on water. He had not healed anyone, and

### Yes, You Should Prefer Others

He had not raised anybody from the dead. *Before* Jesus had done any of these things, He was baptized by His cousin John, and immediately the heavens opened and the Spirit of God descended upon Jesus as God looked down from heaven and said, "This is My beloved Son, with whom I am well pleased" (Matthew 3:17).

There is always a reason to be proud of somebody. God spoke those words for us to hear because He knows people need to be commended for who they are, not just for what they do. Those around you don't need to chalk up thirty-eight accomplishments for you to be proud of them. You can be proud of them just because they are who they are. Think how that would make your spouse feel if he or she heard that from you on a regular basis. How would it make your children feel to hear that you are proud of them? This simple affirmation can mean so much. A kind word, given sincerely, can make a person's day.

In addition to well-chosen words, there are small actions you can do to show others that you regard them more highly than yourself. Even if you're late leaving for work, you can pour your spouse a cup of coffee as you pour yourself one. You may have a long list of things to do, but you can always find a moment to smile at the person beside you or say something upbeat. If someone does something for you, it doesn't take long to say a grateful "Thank you, I really appreciate that." You may think you don't have time to text something encouraging to a friend, but then you find time to scroll on your phone or watch TV. When you give

> **WHEN YOU GIVE FLOWERS (COMPLIMENTS) TO SOMEONE ELSE, IT ALWAYS LEAVES A FRAGRANCE ON YOUR OWN HANDS.**

flowers (compliments) to someone else, it always leaves a fragrance in your own hands.

Something else God has taught me is that He multiplies our time when we take time to help others. If we sacrifice a few moments to do a small act of kindness, God gives us more than enough time to get the other things done. He is pleased when we put others before ourselves and show them that they matter.

Another way to show preference to others is to rejoice with them! Have you noticed, as I have, that we tend to weep together well, but we're not nearly as adept at celebrating others' accomplishments or good news? We're good at rallying around someone who has received sad news. We send texts and emails to pray for the person who is sick or has lost a loved one. We jump to someone's side quickly when there has been abuse or if a friend has received disappointing news. Of course we should continue doing such things in loving support of those we care for. But let's also consider how to respond when someone wins a race. How do I feel when someone else gets a new car—and I've been praying and hoping for one over months and months? What if my friend or colleague got the promotion I think I deserved? If we are honest with ourselves, we sometimes do not genuinely celebrate their achievement with them. We might say nice things and smile, but once we're off to ourselves we question the fairness of life.

To gain a better perspective from someone a little further along in life, here is something I learned from my friend Bill Jones. I remember saying to Bill, "Talk to me about something you've taught your children." In his elementary way Bill shared this pearl of wisdom: "A sign of

*Yes, You Should Prefer Others*

maturity among siblings is when they can revel in their siblings' accomplishments and mean it."

With one of my favorite couples, Bill Jones (left) and his wife, Martha

I have grown to the point where I now get so much more satisfaction when other people succeed than when I succeed. Considering others above yourself helps you show that you care. This is such a hard leadership principle to grasp, but if we want to grow in influence and care for those around us, we need to learn that it is OK for us to decrease so others can increase. When we apply the concepts from part 1 regarding prayer, discipline, and knowing our purpose, we begin to understand that we are living God's will for our lives and trusting that He is in ultimate control. When we are resting more confidently in God's plan for our lives and other people have something to celebrate, we can genuinely celebrate with them. As we grow in confidence of who God created us to be and what He created us

**IT IS OK FOR US TO DECREASE SO OTHERS CAN INCREASE.**

69

to do, we are not looking around and being jealous. We are looking up to our Creator and being grateful.

You honor people and lead well by preferring and celebrating them rather than celebrating yourself. Yes, you can regard others more highly than yourself!

## FOR REFLECTION

1. Reflect on the acronym JOY and what it means. How will remembering to lead with JOY influence your daily interactions from today forward?

2. If leadership is about others, how often do you wake up each day considering how you'll "count others more significant than [yourself]"?

3. Simple things can make a big impact. List three small ways in which you can practice preferring others today.

4. If you've struggled to celebrate others' victories, why? What needs to change in your spirit for you to improve at celebrating others?

## PRINCIPLES TO REMEMBER

- It's OK for us to decrease in order for others to increase.
- Preferring others is letting them know we're proud of them.
- Preferring others is demonstrated through small acts of kindness.
- Preferring others is the ability to sincerely affirm and encourage others.
- Preferring others is being able to celebrate with them their good news or accomplishments.

## PART III

# LEADING THOSE YOU SERVE

*Leadership is not about being in charge.
It's about taking care of those in your charge.*
—Simon Sinek

## CHAPTER 8

# YES, HUMILITY IS REQUIRED

Now we transition to another angle of servant leadership.

In this section we'll talk about upward leadership, or how to best lead those you follow. It's commonly called "managing up." This may look like how an adult son or daughter can lead an aging parent or how you can actually lead a boss.

Even if you are under the authority of someone who is not nice or respectful, you can manage up. You can gently advise and even guide the person above you as he or she forms policy or considers decisions. And I'll tell you right up front: It takes something special on your part—something that doesn't come naturally for most of us.

Remember Philippians 2:3, where Paul instructs us, "Do nothing from selfish ambition or conceit, but in humility count others more significant than yourselves." It holds the other key term that's worthy of our attention: "in humility." Without humility, leaders are more like tyrants. Without humility, they count others *less* significant than themselves, considering themselves the smartest, most important person in the group. They listen less and dictate more. They are no fun to be around. Everything we are talking about in this book requires a daily supply of gentle humility!

When it comes to "managing up," Colossians 3:23 gives great instruction on how to work humbly. "Whatever you do, work heartily, as for the Lord and not for men." No matter what position or role you are in, if you have someone leading you, you can quietly manage up and make an impact right where you are, right now, by working for the Lord! We need to remember that we have only one boss, one superior. If in everything we do we work heartily as to the Lord, our ultimate boss is God!

Everyone is always working for or being held accountable by someone. We all need to be able to receive instruction and submit to the authority of another. I can tell you from experience that this is much easier to do when we remember who our real boss is. This should help us walk in humility and work heartily every moment of every day.

As pastor of our church, I am under the authority of a denomination, a board, and a budget. The best way to lead from this position and influence those above and around me is to lead with humility. I believe there is no room for arrogance among those who work for the Lord. First Corinthians 4:7 reminds us, "What do you have that you did not receive?" Every talent, every success, every gift, every ability has been given to us by God. When we remember that whatever we are doing is a gift from God, there is no room for pride.

Our old friend Nehemiah is a notable example of how to manage up in humility. In Nehemiah 2:5 he said to King Artaxerxes, "If it pleases the king, and if your servant has found favor in your sight...send me to Judah, to the city of my fathers' graves, that I might rebuild it." That's humility.

Nehemiah had heard how vulnerable Jerusalem had become because its wall lay in ruins; he wept, fasted, and prayed. God used his position as a cupbearer to enable him to come humbly before the king.

The right attitude will give you the right access to get the right action.

And that right attitude is humility. Nehemiah reminded the king that he was a servant. He knew he should not ask for anything from the king, but apparently he had done his job well enough for the king to notice that he was downcast. This put Nehemiah in the right place to be heard and for the king to act on God's behalf.

Humility can get us into positions that seem impossible so God can use us for His glory! No matter where we are working or who we are working for, a spirit of gentle humility can put us in a position to do something that honors our Lord. Think of it: Most people, whether followers or leaders, are not compelled to help others who act self-important or entitled. They are much more likely to help someone who leads from true humility. Our humility is to be Christlike: "Take my yoke upon you, and learn from me, for *I am gentle and lowly in heart*" (Matthew 11:29, emphasis added). Jesus described Himself as "gentle and lowly in heart," or truly humble. And He instructed us to "learn from [Him]." If we are going to lead people, especially those in a higher position than we are, we must lead from the position of genuine, Christlike humility—being gentle and lowly in heart.

**THE RIGHT ATTITUDE WILL GIVE YOU THE RIGHT ACCESS TO GET THE RIGHT ACTION.**

Humility will give you longevity in your job. Humility will give you longevity in your marriage. Humility will give you longevity in your friendships. Humility says, "Thank you." Humility is being grateful for where you are and what you have. Humility means doing your job as if you were the boss. Humility is offering others to step ahead of you in line. Humility is looking for ways to care for and serve others rather than looking for ways to take care of yourself first. Humility is being able to recognize that you can learn from anyone!

When we walk in humility, we are thinking of others more than we are thinking of ourselves. We're preferring others over our own self-interests. Said another way, humility is not thinking less of yourself; it's thinking of yourself less!

Paul's writings show how he grew in humility. Watch this! In AD 49, when Paul authored the Book of Galatians, he described himself as "an apostle." About five years later he wrote 1 Corinthians and introduced himself as "the least of the apostles" (15:9). Around five years after that he wrote Ephesians and said he was "the least of all saints" (3:8). Later, Paul wrote 1 Timothy and described himself as the "chief" of sinners (1:15). Did you notice that the further along Paul got in his ministry, the more humbly he described himself?

**HUMILITY IS NOT THINKING LESS OF YOURSELF; IT'S THINKING OF YOURSELF LESS!**

If you want to know if you are progressing in your leadership, notice if you are thinking of yourself less and seeking God's glory more. You (and others) will notice that more of your sentences have fewer personal pronouns. You will have grown in humility, and that makes you more impactful when you have the opportunity to influence those in positions above you!

## Yes, Humility Is Required

One simple way to start exercising humility is to turn a conversation from you to another. Start a conversation by asking the person about their hobbies. Other people love to talk about things that interest them. You may find that you have something in common with them or you may remember that interest the next time you see them. They'll feel valued that you can recall their special interest. You can ask about a recent vacation or plans they may have coming up. You could ask them if they have been anywhere interesting or what places they would most like to visit. You can ask if they work, where they work, or what they enjoy doing for work.

Ask them about their family. You can ask about their spouse or if they have children or grandchildren. You can ask what their family members participate in or what interests them. Most people love to talk about their families, and you can learn so much from them.

Once you get to know people better, you can ask about their faith. (Please do not lead with a faith question. Save this for when you know them better.) If you're not sure if they go to church or what their experience has been with church, you may need to start there. If you have built a relationship and are more comfortable in the relationship, you might ask what they believe. If they don't know Jesus, you may get the opportunity to introduce them to Jesus then or in the future. When you lead relationships in humility, you never know what God has in store!

One of my favorite memories, and a great example of humility, occurred when Barbara and I went to The Cove in Asheville, North Carolina, to visit. Billy Graham's grandson Will picked us up at the airport. Will carried our luggage and put it in his car. He drove us to The Cove, where lunch was being served for a conference. He sat us at a table with his aunt Ann Graham Lotz. But now the table was full, so he went to another table to eat his meal.

Look at the humility Will showed Barbara and me. Later, when we were ready to return home, Will said he had something he wanted to give me. He pulled out a Bible and said, "Benny, this is my grandfather's Bible. Do you remember when I played my grandfather in the movie *Unbroken* two? This is the Bible I used when I was preaching his sermon in the movie."

I told Will I could not take the Bible, that it had been a gift from his grandfather. Will said, "I have the greatest gift. I am William Franklin Graham IV. I have his name." He loaded Barbara and me in the car and drove us back to the airport.

What a beautiful picture of humility in a leader!

Will Graham (right) and me with the Bible he gave me

*Yes, Humility Is Required*

Who would have dreamed that a little boy who came from nothing now owned Billy Graham's Bible? God can use the most unlikely people to do the most extraordinary things! We just need to humble ourselves before Him and others.

Martin Luther said, "God made man out of nothing, and as long as we are nothing, He can make something out of us."[1] I love the poem "The Indispensable Man" by Saxon White Kessinger.[2] I repeat it to myself often to remind me that I am replaceable in most areas of my life, and practicing humility represents God best in every area of my life.

Whether we're managing up, down, or sideways, we're compelled as Christ-followers to lead from a spirit of Christlike humility. This doesn't mean we allow ourselves to get walked on or taken advantage of. It does mean that we don't make ourselves more important than others and that we're willing to learn from everyone. We do our work heartily, as for the Lord. We put our egos aside and serve others willingly, humbly. Humility represents Christ to all those around us.

Yes, you can lead, and it begins with humility.

## FOR REFLECTION

1. As a leader who reports to someone, how well do you receive and act on instructions?
2. On a scale of 1 to 5 (5 = excellent) how would you rate your effectiveness in "managing up" with your leader?
3. As you read the Bible, what specific examples of humility do you see in Jesus?
4. What did you learn from the story of Will Graham that you'd like to emulate this week?

## PRINCIPLES TO REMEMBER

- Humility is the ability to receive instruction from others.
- Humility is the willingness to learn from anyone.
- Humility is being genuinely interested in other people.
- Humility turns conversations from you to others.
- Humility represents Jesus to those around us.

## CHAPTER 9

# YES, MINDSET MATTERS

WHAT YOU THINK about yourself and what you believe about God matters when it comes to leading—especially as you "manage up" with those who lead you.

When you doubt what God can do through you, you diminish how you lead, and God cannot use you to your fullest potential. We must determine that what God says in His Word is true. If God says it, you can believe it. This way of thinking will help your mindset and increase your influence as a leader. Philippians 4:8 tells us: "Finally, brothers, whatever is true, whatever is honorable, whatever is just, whatever is pure, whatever is lovely, whatever is commendable, if there is any excellence, if there is anything worthy of praise, think about these things."

I have knelt on my knees to pray when a terrible thought suddenly entered my mind. I thought to myself, "Where did that thought come from?" I would be embarrassed for you to know some of those thoughts. Second Corinthians 10:5 tells us to "take every thought captive to obey Christ." Romans 12:2 reminds us, "Do not be conformed to this world, but be transformed by the renewal of your mind, that by testing you may discern what is the will of God, what is good and acceptable and perfect." To have the mindset of a good leader, we need to take negative thoughts captive and have Scripture ready to counter the negative thought.

When an unhealthy thought enters your mind, you have a choice whether to entertain that thought. If you entertain it, you may begin to enjoy the thought—and if you're not careful, you may live out the thought. It's hard to positively influence others when you are entertaining negative or impure thoughts. If you're going to lead and care for others, you need to do a checkup from the neck up and get rid of your stinking thinking. Your mindset matters!

There's a plethora of factors that can influence your mindset. If your parents told you, "You are smart" or "You are athletic" or "You are beautiful," you won't have much difficulty believing in yourself. But there's a downside: You may come across as entitled or prideful. If you were raised in an unstable home with people saying negative things about you, your mindset may be unstable; you may believe that you won't amount to much, that you are not worth loving, or that you're not competent to lead anyone or anything. I know this feeling firsthand. My stepfather had little good to say to or about me, which caused me to feel insecure and had me believing I was worthless.

Any extreme of either of these scenarios is not healthy. If you were raised in a home where you were always told you were good, your mindset could be that you are never wrong. Pride can get the best of us. If you were raised in a home where you were told you were worthless, your mindset could be that God could never use you for anything. The truth is, no matter which scenario was part of your formative years, God can use you. His Holy Spirit within you is able to overrule your unhealthy past and renew your mind with the knowledge that you are God's creation. He has filled you with His power to accomplish great things for His glory.

To me, one of the saddest stories in the Bible is found in 1 Samuel 16, where God said to Samuel, "I will send you to Jesse the Bethlehemite, for I have selected for myself a king among his sons." Jesse presented seven of his sons to Samuel, but the Lord did not choose any of the seven. Finally, Samuel asked Jesse, "Are all your sons here?" Jesse had not mentioned David, never considered young David a worthy candidate. Jesse saw a shepherd boy, but God saw a king! People consider the outward appearance, but God sees the heart.

In 1 Samuel 17, Israel's army was at war with the Philistines. David's three oldest brothers were there, so one day Jesse sent David to take food to his brothers. It didn't take long for David to realize that Israel's soldiers and king were huddled in camp, trembling at the thought of fighting the gargantuan Philistine champion. As Goliath belligerently mocked God and the Israelites, David asked a nearby soldier, "What shall be done for the man who kills this Philistine and takes away the reproach from Israel? For who is this uncircumcised Philistine, that he should defy the armies of the living God?" (v. 26).

**JESSE SAW A SHEPHERD BOY, BUT GOD SAW A KING!**

When David's oldest brother heard what he was asking, he reminded young David that he was supposed to be tending sheep and falsely accused him of coming just to "see the battle" (v. 28). But soon David told King Saul that he would go up against the giant. Saul said, "You are not able to go against this Philistine to fight with him, for you are but a youth, and he has been a man of war from his youth." David replied, "Your servant used to keep sheep for his father. And when there came a lion, or a bear, and took a lamb from the flock, I went after him and struck him and delivered it out of his mouth....Your servant has struck down both lions and bears, and this uncircumcised Philistine shall be like one of them, for he has defied the armies of the living God" (vv. 33–36).

David did not stop there. His mindset was on what God could do. He told King Saul, confidently, "The LORD who delivered me from the paw of the lion and from the paw of the bear will deliver me from the hand of this Philistine" (v. 37). Do you see David's mindset despite what his father and brothers thought about him? Do you see David's mindset despite Saul observing that he was only a "youth"? David chose to trust God. This young man knew God, and he remembered what God had done in his life. David did not listen to what others said he should be doing or what others thought he should be. He was confident that God would save him and deliver him in battle, and he chose to believe that truth. Soon, in the name of God and Israel, this bold teenager slew Goliath with a slingshot and a stone. How had he convinced Saul to let him fight Goliath? David had the mindset that with God, all things are possible.

Today you may feel like you were never picked, never chosen, or never gifted, talented, or good-looking enough. You got passed over for a raise you felt you deserved. Your spouse let you down. Your church isn't growing. Your children aren't behaving as they should. There are times when you feel so bad about yourself, when you feel you just don't measure up. I want to encourage you to never doubt what God can do through you! Remember, when God saw a

*Yes, Mindset Matters*

shepherd boy, He saw a king! If God can use someone like David, and if He can use someone like me, then He can absolutely use someone like you to do extraordinary things for Him! All you need is a can-do mindset that believes God actually, really, wants to do His work through us.

One of my modern-day heroes in the faith is Tommy Barnett. He is the pastor of one of the largest Assemblies of God churches in the United States. Tommy cofounded the Dream Center in Los Angeles, is chancellor of Southeastern University, serves on boards of large ministries, and has authored many books. Once I asked him, "If you could do your ministry over, what would you do differently?" And Tommy responded, "I would dream bigger. If I had dreamed bigger, God would've done more!"

**NEVER DOUBT WHAT GOD CAN DO THROUGH YOU!**

A dreamer and spiritual giant, Tommy Barnett (right)

I consider Tommy's life and think, "He has accomplished so much!" But Tommy reminded me of Ephesians 3:20: "Now to him who is able to do far more abundantly than all that we ask or think, according to the power at work within us." When we ask for more, God can do so much more! Our mindset matters, and our mindset should be that God can do far more in us than we can ever do on our own.

A positive mindset will produce positive results in your life. William James said, "Thoughts become perception, perception becomes reality. Alter your thoughts, alter your reality."[1] We have little control over the circumstances in our lives, but we can control our mindsets. Many times, things do not turn out the way we planned. Sometimes relationships don't work out as we'd hoped. Sometimes, in spite of our prayers and hard work, our children don't come out as we'd hoped. Sometimes our jobs or careers or finances don't work out the way we'd planned. We cannot determine what happens *to* us, but we can determine what happens *in* us.

A positive mindset begins with the will. David is such a great example for us that I'll tell another story about him. After Goliath's death, Saul made David one of his warriors, and David won many battles. In fact, the Israelite women would dance at David's victorious return, singing "Saul has struck down his thousands, and David his ten thousands" (1 Samuel 18:7). This turned Saul's heart to jealous, raging hatred against David, and the young man had to flee for his life.

For several years David had to hide in caves and dodge Saul's armies. In the midst of his difficulties David wrote: "I will bless the Lord at all times; his praise shall continually be in my mouth" (Psalm 34:1). David chose a positive, God-trusting mindset during his most difficult times. A positive mindset starts with the will and then flows to your emotions. In the next verse he wrote, "My soul shall make its boast in the LORD."

David is showing us that a positive mindset affects how we feel. A positive mindset also has an uplifting effect on those we lead. Psalm 34:3 says, "Oh, magnify the LORD with me, and let us exalt His name *together*" (emphasis added). It starts with our will, flows to our emotions, and then flows to those we influence.

When it comes to keeping a positive mindset, we must remember that we are God's children. If we are not confident that we are deeply loved by Him, our effectiveness as leaders will be limited. If we are not sure of our purpose or how God feels about us, we may allow insecurity to take over and attempt to lead by me-first instead of others-first principles.

Insecurities are easy to spot in others but more difficult to spot in ourselves. If we try to lead our spouse from a mindset of insecurity, we may become micromanagers or control freaks and suffocate those we love most. If we attempt to lead our children from a mindset of insecurity, we may parent from a stance of fear and overprotectiveness. If we try to lead coworkers from insecurity, we may be defensive and distrustful. When any of us have a tough time complimenting or giving credit to other people, we're leading from insecurity. If we hold a gnawing inner need for commendation or praise, we're leading from insecurity.

We need a mindset shift. We need to shift our minds away from what we feel we lack and focus on our true identity in Jesus Christ. We need to ask God, through His

Holy Spirit, to renew our minds so we'll cease seeking our sense of worth in people, position, or performance. We need to look to the One who provides us with our worth in Him.

When we have a mindset of who we are in Christ, we do not mind when other people get the credit or praise; we can rejoice and celebrate with them. When we know who we are in Jesus, we don't mind celebrating others' victories. We know that when one member of our family or team gets better, we all do. When we have a mindset of caring for others, we don't need to micromanage every detail for those we are with. We need to know who we are in Christ and remember that what He thinks about us is more important than what other people say to us or about us. When our mindset is on the things of God, our families, coworkers, organizations, and ministries become unlimited in what can be accomplished for the heavenly kingdom!

> **WE NEED TO LOOK TO THE ONE WHO PROVIDES US WITH OUR WORTH IN HIM.**

Your mindset is where you find true security. You may be asking yourself, "Benny, how do you develop a mindset of security in leadership?" I'll tell you what I have learned. Your self-worth must be in Christ. Everything else is going to pass. You were made in the image of God, and your identity is in Him! When you are confident of your identity being in Christ, your mindset is set on things above and your ability to lead, influence, and care for others rises to another level. Anyone can have a relationship with God and have their identity in Him. You will be a better person to everyone around you if you know you are His child and you seek to reflect His image in all you do.

*Yes, Mindset Matters*

You are a child of God!

Let me tell you about a man named Ben. Ben was born to an unwed mother. He had a challenging time growing up because every place he went, he was always asked, "Hey, boy, who's your daddy?" Whether he was at school, in the grocery or drug store, or elsewhere, people would ask the same question. "Who's your daddy?" Ben would hide from other students at recess and lunchtime. He would avoid going into stores because the question always hurt him.

When he was about twelve, a new preacher came to his church. The boy would always go in late and slip out early to avoid facing the question, "Who's your daddy?" But one day the new preacher said the benediction so fast that Ben did not have time to leave the church before the preacher finished; he had to walk out with the crowd. About the time Ben reached the back door, the preacher put his hand on the boy's shoulder and asked him, "Son, who's your daddy?"

Everyone around got deathly quiet. Ben could feel every eye looking at him. By now everyone else knew the answer to the question, "Who's your daddy?" This new preacher, though, sensed the awkward situation around him. With discernment that only the Holy Spirit can give, he said to that scared little boy, "Wait a minute! I know who you are! I see the family resemblance now. You are a child of God."

With that the wise preacher patted Ben on the shoulder and said, "Boy, you have a great inheritance. Go and claim it." With that, the boy smiled for the first time in a long time and left the church a changed person. He was never the same again. Whenever anybody asked him, "Who's your daddy?" he would just tell them, "I'm a child of God."[2]

This young boy was Ben Hooper, who grew up to be governor of Tennessee!

When you know whose you are, you are in a beautiful place to serve, care, and lead others with confidence. Whether you're a spouse, parent, employee, employer, an addict, an inmate, someone isolated, or someone who needs healing, you are a child of God—and He loves you unconditionally!

Your mindset does matter, and you get to choose your mindset.

I want to wrap this chapter by sharing a few ways to keep a positive mindset when leading others.

First, be grateful. God has been so good to us; we should never run out of things to be grateful for. Gratitude always begets a positive mindset. Consider Psalm 118:23–24: "This is the LORD's doing; it is marvelous in our eyes. This is the day the LORD has made; let us rejoice and be glad in it." We become grateful when we realize what God has done, what He is doing, and what He is going to do for us.

**YOUR MINDSET DOES MATTER, AND YOU GET TO CHOOSE YOUR MINDSET.**

One of the ways I practice gratitude is what I call "Reverse Thanksgiving." I'll pray, "God, I thank You that I don't have a bad job. Thank You that I have a good job." Or "God, I thank You that my retinas are not torn or detached. I thank You that I can see to the back row of our auditorium." Or "Thank You that I don't have shingles like I did last Easter and that my body is whole." Or "I thank You, God, that I have a warm bed and a warm car when it is cold outside." And "I thank You I don't have a nagging wife. Barbara is a such a wonderful wife and life partner."

You might want to try this—it works wonders!

Another great way to maintain a positive mindset is to apply what we've emphasized from the start of this book: Focus more on other people, just as Jesus did. I try to keep in mind Paul's instruction to "Do nothing from selfish ambition or conceit, but *in humility count others more significant than yourselves*. Let each of you look not only to his own interests, but also to the interests of others. Have this mind among yourselves, which is yours in Christ Jesus" (Philippians 2:3–5, emphasis added).

I recall reading that most people think about themselves 95 percent of the time. That statistic isn't scientific but it reveals a truth: People spend a lot of time thinking about themselves. We need to turn that around! If we'll have the Spirit-led courage to become more focused on others, we will be more like Jesus! The change of mindset will revolutionize our lives and our leadership.

I'll share one last way to attain and maintain a positive mindset: Surround yourself with positive Christ followers. You are influenced by those closest to you. There's an old story about a guy who entered his mule in the Kentucky Derby. When asked why, he replied, "I thought the association would do him a world of good." People with negative mindsets often surround themselves with negative people. Those with positive mindsets seek out others with positive mindsets. A negative outlook is highly contagious, but so is a positive outlook! Spending most of your time with upbeat people helps nurture and strengthen your positive, can-do mindset.

I want you to know, there have been many days when I have been disappointed in myself. Days when I didn't like myself or even want to get out of bed. The truth is that my mindset was dismal. I've learned that an upbeat outlook is something I need to practice daily. It takes discipline. So what I want you to understand is this: God loves you and me unconditionally! We have not always loved Him unconditionally, but He has *always* loved you and me unconditionally. God is your daddy. You belong to Him! Find your identity in Him daily, and seek to honor Him each day. Seek His heart in your everyday details. When you can grasp the reality that the Creator of the universe loves you, you'll be empowered to impact anyone for His glory!

Yes, your mindset matters!

## FOR REFLECTION

1. What were things adults said to you as a child that still influence your mindset today?

2. Of the things spoken to you as a child, which ones does God say are true about you?

3. What practices do you have in place to live by a positive mindset? If this area of your life could be stronger, what Scripture will you memorize to encourage a positive outlook?

4. If you were to see yourself as a child of God, how would that change the way you lead?

5. People don't perform at their best when following an insecure leader. What can you do to eliminate insecurity from your life?

6. What are truths the Bible says about you that can help you carry a positive mindset?

## PRINCIPLES TO REMEMBER

- Your mindset needs to be fixed on what God says is true.

- Your mindset should be that the Creator of the universe deeply loves you.

- Your mindset should be that your worth is in Jesus, not in positions, achievements, or things.

- Your mindset should be that you are a child of God, made in His image.

- Your mindset should be to care for others more than yourself.
- Your mindset will be more upbeat if you are grateful.
- Your mindset will be more positive if you surround yourself with positive people.

# CHAPTER 10

# YES, PRIORITIES MATTER

WE CANNOT TAKE our family, our job, or our everyday life to the next level if we don't know what our priorities are. I've found that there are three key questions we need to ask if we are to live and lead with a proper sense of what matters most:

1. First, who is my master?
2. Second, who is my mate?
3. Third, what is my mission?

I believe that, as a leader, your number one priority must be your love for God. It's elementary yet profound. Matthew 6:33 says, "But seek first the kingdom of God and his righteousness, and all these things will be added to you." In other words, God must be number one in your life. He is to be top priority—always.

When we are in a position to lead our families, peers, coworkers, or even our bosses, it's so easy to get caught up in what others think of us or how others will respond to us. But when we have made God our top priority and we trust Him, we are making leadership decisions based on what *He* thinks of us.

So who is your God?

If your god is money, you'll make decisions based on how to make the next dollar. You may be tempted to cheat on taxes or fudge a financial arrangement. If your god is dating, you will make decisions based on how to attract the person you are enamored with at the moment. Decisions based on the worship of dating may cost you your family, your money, and your self-respect. If your god is alcohol, gambling, or drugs, you'll make decisions that can cost you your life savings, your family, your freedom, or your life.

But if your God is the Creator of the universe and His Son, Jesus Christ, you will make decisions based on God's guidance. If He is who you worship, you'll make decisions that enable you to live in peace, without regret, and freedom like you've never experienced before. If you want to lead at the next level, you'll need to make the crucial decision to make God your number one priority. I cannot promise you a raise or a promotion or a better marriage or perfect children. What I can promise is that if you prioritize God in your life, your outlook will be more upbeat, caring, full of faith, and filled with peace.

**IF YOU PRIORITIZE GOD IN YOUR LIFE, YOUR OUTLOOK WILL BE FILLED WITH PEACE.**

When your outlook becomes more positive and you carry God's peace about you, you no longer look for the promotion or next big thing; you begin to look for God's will to be done, not yours. God will give you a life full of Him! Nothing is better than that. Yes, you can ask God to be Lord of your life!

Your next priority should be your spouse and your family. No one at home should feel that they are competing with anyone or anything else for your love and attention. They should never feel that your job, your cell phone, your extended family, or your hobbies take priority over them.

I must confess that I have not always gotten this right with my family. I regret the days that I put my mission above my time with my wife and daughter. There have been times when I have gotten exciting news and told everyone around me before I told my wife. By the time I got home and told her the news, I was not as excited anymore. I decided to make Barbara my priority, and when something wonderful happens in my life, I call her first. I want her to get the best of what happens in my life.

It was a momentous day in my life when I realized that the Church is Jesus' bride and Barbara is my bride. I have seen times when adults have inappropriate relationships with their jobs. The relationship may not be with a person, but with an organization, friends, or extracurricular activities. I will never forget a trip I was able to take in 2011. I went to Montreat, North Carolina, and sat down with Billy Graham. I asked him questions and took notes. The last question I asked him, "Talk to me about regrets and the things you would do differently." I wrote down what he said: "I would speak less and study more. I would spend more time with my family. Every day I was absent from my family is gone forever."

Being in the ministry, I have had the opportunity to comfort men when they die. What is amazing to me when I am in that place is that none of them have ever talked about their accomplishments or material possessions. What they want to talk about in their last days is being with their families. The point I want all of us to understand is this: If it can happen to Billy Graham, it can happen to any of us.

I know there is talk from "experts" about work/life balance. I don't believe there is any such thing as complete balance. There are those of us who tend to get out of balance depending on what life challenges we have in any given season. I want to encourage us all to be aware when we are out of balance and work to keep God and family our priorities.

Your third priority is your mission. Your mission is where you choose to go out and share your faith with the world. It could be your job, a ministry, coworkers, friends, or a church. What I know is that if you have chosen your mission and you love what you're doing, you will succeed in what you put your mind to. If you enjoy where you spend your time, others will be drawn to Jesus. In 1 Thessalonians 2:8 Paul wrote, "Because we loved you so much, we were dedicated to share with you not only the gospel of God, but our lives as well" (NIV). When choosing your mission, choose something you enjoy. Don't spend your entire life doing something that you do not take pleasure in doing. I am not telling you to walk to your boss right now and quit. I am saying that you need to begin finding something you love and pursue that. Man's greatest happiness is achieved when his work and play become inseparable. Successful leaders love what they are doing.

**MAN'S GREATEST HAPPINESS IS ACHIEVED WHEN HIS WORK AND PLAY BECOME INSEPARABLE.**

Even in your mission, you need to make sure you keep the main thing the main thing. If you are working for someone and you would like to know what your priorities should be, let me help. The first thing your leader wants to see is for you to view your job as if you owned the business. There is a difference between a person who comes to work for a paycheck and a person who comes to "work heartily, as for the Lord and not for men" (Colossians 3:23). If you go to work and make it your priority to work as if you're the boss and you're trying to please God, you will go the extra mile. You will see things no one else sees. You will do things others don't want to do. You may be thinking, "Benny, if I do that, I'll be doing more and not getting paid for it!" And you may be right. I can also tell you that when people work like that in my organization, they get noticed, and they end up getting paid what they are worth. If your mindset is that you work for the Lord, He requires you to work heartily and cheerfully. You'll be a much better team member when you work as God wants you to work.

Your boss would like you to steward your time, budget, materials, resources, and relationships as if you were paying the bills. This idea of stewardship is biblical. "Moreover, it is required of stewards that they be found faithful" (1 Corinthians 4:2). Be mindful of how you spend the company money and treat the company assets. Be mindful of lights or air conditioning being left on when no one is in the room or building. Don't waste time or resources. If you punch a time clock, don't clock in and then do personal things before you begin working. By treating your workplace as if you own it, you are pleasing the Lord and caring for your boss. You can be a leader by showing great stewardship.

Your leader also appreciates it when you continue to develop your awareness and skills. If you don't want the organization to outgrow you, continue to develop personally. You could learn or enhance your skills online. You can read books and listen to podcasts about your trade or industry. By committing to ongoing personal development, you enable yourself to lead others at an up-to-date, informed new level.

Whether supporting your boss or leading where you are, keeping your priorities in order is vital to leadership success. In reference to distractions, keep in mind: "You will never reach your destination if you stop and throw stones at every dog that barks."

Again, Nehemiah gives us a fitting example. In Nehemiah 6, we find him rebuilding Jerusalem's wall as his enemies try multiple dirty tricks to stop or distract him from the job. In one attempt they invited him to take a break from work and meet with them. Nehemiah replied, "I am doing a great work and I cannot come down. Why should the work stop while I leave it and come down to you?" (v. 3).

**KEEPING YOUR PRIORITIES IN ORDER IS VITAL TO LEADERSHIP SUCCESS.**

We need to be ready for the enemy's attempts to distract and keep us from doing our best work. If Nehemiah hadn't known his priorities, he could have been distracted from the important task. Without a complete wall, Jerusalem would have been in danger. People living in Jerusalem would not have been safe. There are always negative consequences to not having our priorities in proper order. Fortunately, Nehemiah put the Lord first every day, and God gave him the passion, focus, and wisdom to lead others in completing the work.

If our priorities are in order, we too will put God first

in our day. If we invite Him to guide us every second of every day, we'll know if and when the enemy is distracting us to keep us from God's will. Sure, not every day can be perfect, and there are emergencies that come up. But often we can look at a distraction and say with Nehemiah, "I am doing a great work, and I cannot come down."

Yes, you can lead well by keeping your priorities in order!

## FOR REFLECTION

1. We often think of priorities as a to-do list, when we chase after the *urgent* instead the *important*. What are your current priorities as a leader? How do they dictate your typical day?

2. I recommend that our priorities should be (1) your Master, (2) your mate, and (3) your mission. How would adopting these make a difference in how you work and lead?

3. If God is your Master, in what ways do you make Him your number one priority every day? How will you do better?

4. Something that comes up unexpectedly can quickly become an urgent priority. What can you do to make sure your mate knows he or she is still the most important person in your life, regardless of what is happening?

## PRINCIPLES TO REMEMBER

- Your priorities are Master, mate, and mission.
- Put God first in everything you do.
- Your spouse should never feel that they are considered last in your day.
- Your children deserve your loving time and attention.
- When you enjoy what you are doing, others want to be a part of your mission.

## PART IV

# LEADING THOSE ENTRUSTED TO YOUR CARE

*You can have everything in life you want, if you will just help enough other people get what they want.*
—Zig Ziglar

## CHAPTER 11

# YES, YOU SHOULD CAST A CLEAR VISION

As THE LEADER of your family or team, you will sometimes wake up and discover that things are not going so well. You begin looking for someone to blame but rightly conclude that the one to blame is the person in your mirror. This has happened to me more times than I have space to write about.

Rock Springs Church is not my first church; it is my third. My first church was Mountain Crest Church on Harrison Ferry Mountain, Tennessee. Friends, I did such a wonderful job leading that church that it closed after I left to pastor my next church. I don't consider that good leadership; I consider it a failure. The second church I pastored was Sweeton Hill Church in Coalmont, Tennessee. I often say I stayed there three years and left for health reasons—the deacons got sick of me.

I started at Sweeton Hill after the deacons voted me in 7 to 6. The guy who broke the tie said he hoped I would do good. While I was there, the church grew to three hundred people, but I built a crowd, not a congregation. The church declined quickly after I left. When I go back and visit the church, it saddens me. Sweeton Hill was built on my energy, personality, and enthusiasm, not on leading and growing a congregation. In both churches, I felt like a failure.

But your pain can drive your passion.

As I nursed my self-inflicted wounds, the Lord showed me that there were things I didn't know that would have made me a better leader. I began to process what I could do better or differently at Rock Springs. First, the Holy Spirit showed me that I needed to develop a clear, Christ-inspired vision that others would buy into and be inspired to follow.

Proverbs 29:18 says, "Where there is no vision, the people perish" (KJV). If you are a pastor, I'll say it this way: "Where there is no vision, the people will find another parish." If you're a husband and/or parent, "Where there is no vision, the family will seek others to follow." As a leader in any capacity, there are things others can do that you don't need to be doing, and there are things that you cannot delegate. You cannot delegate casting a vision. That is your responsibility. If you tell me you are only leading a Sunday school class, I'll tell you that you need a vision for your class. If you are the leader of the home, you should cast a vision for the family. If you lead a business or a team, you need to cast a vision for those who follow you. I love what Cavett Robert said: "When it's foggy in the pulpit, it's cloudy in the pew."[1]

**YOU CANNOT DELEGATE CASTING A VISION. THAT IS YOUR RESPONSIBILITY.**

This is true for any organization or home. If the leader does not know where he or she wants to go, those following are just following blindly or will look for someone else to follow.

*Yes, You Should Cast a Clear Vision*

No one can have a better vision for your family than you. No one can have a better vision for your team at work and where your organization is going than you. It is imperative that you, as a leader, are spending time with God and seeking Christ-inspired vision. "What is Your vision for my family? What is Your vision for my team?" I believe that God will give vision to the leader who humbles himself before Him. I don't think God limits vision to those in corporate leadership, pastors, or business owners. He gives vision to anyone who seeks Him and asks Him for it.

I also believe that if you have a vision, you need to make it "catchable." God will give Mom and Dad a vision for the home, but Mom and Dad need to make the vision clear enough—and exciting enough—for the children to follow.

I spent years letting other people make their vision my vision; I was not wise enough to seek and articulate my own vision. I came to realize that God had called *them* to do what they were telling *me* to do. He had not called me to do that. How do you know what the vision is for you?

**YOUR VISION WILL OFTEN ARISE FROM YOUR BURDEN.**

You walk closely with the Lord and seek His guidance. Interestingly, the word for *oracle* in Hebrew can be translated as "burden."[2] God will place a special burden on your heart, much as He did with our friend Nehemiah. And your vision will often arise from your burden.

Why did I start a home for pregnant, unmarried girls? Well, when my mother was pregnant with me, she had no husband or anyone to support her. Years later, the Lord burdened my heart for pregnant, unmarried girls who needed a place of respite. It wasn't long before we launched

Melba's Manor to love, care for, and support hundreds of girls and young women.

Why does Rock Springs Church have three medical clinics offering free health care? Well, I had spent years with no insurance and no way to pay for medical care, and now I could see hundreds of people in our area who also had no means to obtain good care. My vision came from my burden.

Too many people in positions of leadership don't know where they're going. If you are one of those leaders, I want to encourage you to seek out the vision God has for you, find what burdens you, and allow Him to form the vision in your heart.

Once you have a vision, there are things you should do to communicate the vision to those you lead. Habakkuk 2:2 says, "Write the vision; make it plain on tablets." Makes sense. If the vision is misty to the leader, it will be foggy to the followers. Once we have the vision, there are several things we can do to build consensus and buy-in.

**State the vision clearly.** Write down the vision and then simplify it so it is clear, easy to understand, and memorable. I once heard a story about a military commander who was known for being especially effective. It turns out that whenever he had a vision he wanted to communicate to his followers, he would ask that a certain man with learning challenges be brought to his tent. The commander would share his vision with this man and then ask him to repeat what had just been shared. The commander knew that if this particular person could understand what he wanted to communicate, then everyone else should be able to get it.

You must state the vision clearly. Unclouded vision leads to common ground. You've clearly conveyed your vision when your followers understand it and are enthusiastic about seeing it through. Yes, you can cast a clear vision!

**Repeat the vision constantly.** Once you have the vision and there is clarity with those you lead, find creative ways to keep the vision in front of them—early and often.

Once, Truett Cathy, founder of Chick-fil-A, stayed at a Ritz-Carlton. He noticed that it made him feel good whenever he said, "Thank you" and the Ritz staff replied, "My pleasure!" So Truett developed a vision: When a customer visited any Chick-fil-A restaurant and said, "Thank you," his team members would respond, "My pleasure!" How did Cathy implement this? At an annual meeting, he took the stage and had everyone practice it. Every year after that conference, Cathy would emphasize the vision and have managers and staff practice the cordial interaction.

When I eat at a Chick-fil-A today and say, "Thank you," most team members reply, "My pleasure!" That's what happens when a vision is stated clearly and repeated regularly. And vision leaks. You'll know that your vision is coming to fruition when others in your family or on your team begin citing the vision themselves.

**Celebrate the vision regularly.** We must celebrate what we want more of. If you've conveyed the vision and you catch someone putting the vision into practice, make sure you acknowledge that you see it. Thank that person for displaying the behavior that supports the vision you cast. Offer a high-five or have a small token ready to hand out in celebration. This encourages others to invest in the vision and make it a reality.

**Embrace the vision personally.** Good leadership is monkey see, monkey do. You do not teach what you do not know, and you do not lead where you will not go.

Nehemiah displayed so many great qualities of a leader. His burden had become his vision. Remember how he first cast his vision to King Artaxerxes? In Nehemiah 2:5 we read, "And I said to the king, 'If it pleases the king, and if your servant has found favor in your sight, that you send me to Judah, to the city of my fathers' graves, that I may rebuild it.'"

Later, he would cast the same vision to the priests, nobles, officials, and other workers. "Then I said to them, 'You see the trouble we are in, how Jerusalem lies in ruins with its gates burned. Come, let us rebuild the wall of Jerusalem, that we may no longer suffer derision.' And I told them of the hand of my God that had been upon me for good, and also of the words that the king had spoken to me. And they said, 'Let us rise up and build.' So they strengthened their hands for the good work" (Nehemiah 2:17–18).

Nehemiah embraced the vision personally—so strongly that the king and many others were willing to support and participate in his mission. When the enemy came against them, he reminded the people that God would fight for them because the vision was to get the wall of Jerusalem rebuilt. When people were doubting, Nehemiah retold the vision. When they were in danger, Nehemiah reminded them of God's strength and care.

We're told in Nehemiah 1 that only the remnants of the Jewish nation were still in Jerusalem. These were the people Babylon had not considered pretty, handsome, smart, or gifted. They had been left behind, and not one of them ever had a vision to rebuild Jerusalem's wall. But Nehemiah took that remnant and built the wall in just fifty-two days! It took a leader to embrace the vision, cast it for others, organize and motivate workers, and work alongside them.

When you embrace your own vision, you can review it with those you lead no matter the circumstances or challenges you face. When you have a vision, God can give you a mere "remnant" to work with and accomplish extraordinary things for His glory! When you embrace your vision, others will want to join you in the work. Make sure you communicate your vision clearly to those you lead and repeat it often. Celebrate when others take steps that help fulfill the vision. Embrace your vision fully, so you can review it in challenging seasons and encourage others to embrace it with you.

God does not call the equipped; He equips the called. Your family, your team, your ministry, and your friends all want to be a part of something bigger than they are. Vision helps meet that inner need. It motivates! If God could use "unlikely" people like a cupbearer and a bunch of remnant rejects to rebuild the wall of Jerusalem, He can use the unlikely today to do great works for Him.

And He will—by giving you and your people a vision.

## FOR REFLECTION

1. What is the vision you cast for those you lead?
2. How will you know that the people you lead know and understand your vision?
3. How often do you mention your vision? Is it often enough? Too often?
4. How do others know that you personally embrace the vision?
5. When you see someone helping move your vision forward, how will you celebrate them?

## PRINCIPLES TO REMEMBER

- Where there is no vision, the people perish.
- No one can have a better vision for your life than you.
- Often, your vision will arise from your burden. What are you burdened for?
- Ask God to show you His vision for your life.
- Once you have a vision, be sure you state the vision clearly.
- Cast your vision regularly and repeat it often.
- Celebrate the success of the vision!

## CHAPTER 12

# YES, YOU CAN EMPOWER OTHERS

I F I DO it all by myself, I won't have anyone to high-five. We all need a team. Even the Lone Ranger had Tonto. I spent years attempting to build a church on my own. In the early days, I opened the church. I folded the bulletins myself. I felt that I needed to be the one who closed the church up, do all of the hospital visits, and make every decision alone. There were things I was doing that I enjoyed, but I realized that if I was doing *all* the things, I was hurting the organization, wearing myself out, and not allowing other people to develop their abilities. Finally, I said to myself, "I cannot do this anymore. I want to do more, but I cannot do it by myself anymore. The only way I can lead others better and care for people better is by imparting responsibility to others close to me and pouring into them."

What I learned was that doing it all alone was hard, exhausting, and lonely. God did not create us to be alone or do things alone. I learned that it is imperative for leaders to let go of some details or tasks and empower others to take them on. Not only did this lighten my load and help me be a better-balanced person, but it also gave others the joy of serving and growing.

In 1969, Neil Armstrong became the first man to step on the moon. It took four hundred thousand people working behind the scenes to make that first step happen.[1] Armstrong could never have made it to the moon if he had not trusted people to do what they were trained and skilled to do.

There was a time when I didn't know I wasn't a good writer. I wrote two little ol' books myself—every word. They did not sell well. Now I ask skilled writers to help me author my books. As I have gradually learned to let go and become more dependent on other people in areas where I'm not gifted, my load has become manageable, my faith has developed, and those who have stepped up to take on some ministry tasks have grown spiritually as they minister to others. Our church can accomplish more for the kingdom of God, and if we do things together, there is not much we cannot accomplish.

As we continue to follow Nehemiah in our study of leadership, let's remember that there had been people living in Jerusalem before Nehemiah got there, but they had done nothing to rebuild the wall. Nehemiah came in energized and inspired, and he mobilized them to help him do the work. Nehemiah 2:19 tells us, "But when Sanballat the Horonite and Tobiah the Ammonite servant and Geshem the Arab heard of it, they jeered at us and despised us and said, 'What is this thing that you are doing? Are you rebelling against the king?'" Here we see Nehemiah immediately confronted with opposition and ridicule. He had personally embraced the vision. He knew he could not do the huge job himself, so he conveyed the vision clearly to Jerusalem's remnant residents. They too caught the vision! But they worked under threat of physical attack from outsiders who opposed the project. So, as Nehemiah 4:16–17 tells us, "From that day on, half of my servants worked on construction, and half held the spears, shields, bows, and coats of mail. And the leaders stood behind the whole house of Judah, who were building on the wall."

Nehemiah gave his workers specific roles. There were people building the wall, and there were men protecting everyone else against their enemies. Some people mixed mortar, some carried rocks. Nehemiah displayed the leadership qualities of delegation and empowerment. One of the reasons God puts you in a position to lead is so you can assign others specific roles, then empower them to succeed in their roles. This enables you to focus on the things only you can do.

Let's take a moment to look at another "unlikely" leader in the Bible: Moses.

Moses was born in Egypt shortly after the Pharoah had decided that the Hebrew population was growing too rapidly and could take over his kingdom. Pharoah ordered that all midwives who delivered a Hebrew boy must kill it by throwing the baby in the river. Moses' mom was able to keep him hidden for three months, then she placed him in a basket and launched him into the Nile River, hoping he would be found and saved. The child was found by Pharoah's daughter, and his life was spared. He was raised as a grandson of Pharoah.

When he was older, Moses killed an Egyptian overseer for abusing a Hebrew slave.

He fled into the wilderness, became a shepherd, and married a shepherdess. But God was not done with Moses. After forty years, He called this unlikely shepherd to return to Egypt, approach Pharaoh, and tell him to let God's people go.

Moses resisted, explaining to God that he had a stutter (as if God didn't already know) and was not the right person to undertake this mission. But God uses the unlikely. He told Moses that his Hebrew biological brother, Aaron, would speak for him. They'd be a team. So Moses obeyed God and led the children of Israel out of Egypt toward the Promised Land.

While leading the masses through the wilderness, Moses had taken on the responsibility for mediating their many conflicts and disputes. Consider your experiences dealing with conflicts among your family and coworkers and multiply them by ten thousand. It's no wonder Moses' father-in-law, Jethro, wisely pulled him aside and said, "What you are doing is not good. You and the people with you will certainly wear yourselves out, for the [task] is too heavy for you. You are not able to do it alone" (Exodus 18:17–18).

Jethro saw that Moses was getting exhausted trying to tackle all the disputes by himself. What he then advised Moses to do was Leadership 101—just as timely for leaders today as it was then. Here's my personal summary of Jethro's wise counsel from Exodus 18:19–22:

- Invite God in to help you make the right decisions for those you lead. Jethro said, "I will give you advice, and God be with you! You shall represent the people before God and bring their cases to God."

- How do we select good people to help us lead, and what qualifies them to assume authority? Jethro said, "Moreover, look for able men from all the people, men who fear God, who are trustworthy and hate a bribe, and place such men over the people as chiefs of thousands, of hundreds, of fifties, and of tens."

- What roles should the new leadership team fill? Jethro advised, "Let them judge the people at all times. Every great matter they shall bring to you, but any small matter they shall decide themselves."

What should you and I do to build a better family, organization, workplace environment, community, or ministry—and not wear ourselves out in the process?

Surround yourself with good people and delegate. Empower them to lighten your load as Nehemiah and Moses did. Look for people who are obedient to God's will for their lives. The fear of the Lord should be the paramount qualification for leadership in your home, workplace, or circle of influence. Proverbs 9:10 says, "The fear of the LORD is the beginning of wisdom." Settle for nothing less and aspire to nothing more. When you select others who love the Lord and are obedient to Him, you will be choosing men and women with values in harmony with your own.

I also believe leaders should surround themselves with people who believe in them. As I look back over my time as a leader, husband, father, and friend, I can think of one person who has believed in me more than I believed in myself. My wife, Barbara. Because of my past, I have battled low self-esteem, and Barbara has been the wind beneath my wings. She believes I can do anything. She is the only person who has my best interest at heart at all times. If you are single and looking for a spouse, make sure you look for someone who loves the Lord first and who also believes in you. When I am looking around for people to help achieve the vision God has entrusted to me, I go to Barbara first. Why first? She's my most trusted confidant and adviser. She has the gifts of prayer and discernment, and she helps me discern who God would have me choose for my inner circle. It is important to delegate responsibilities to others, but we need to be wise with whom we choose to fill those positions. Those who believe in us will help pick us up when situations get hard.

**CHARACTER ALWAYS QUALIFIES AUTHORITY IN THE KINGDOM OF GOD.**

Once I realized the need to surround myself with other godly people, I began looking for those with the character qualities and work ethic I desired in our church. Character always qualifies authority in the kingdom of God.

To anyone we influence and care for, we are always Jesus' representatives. If you are a parent, you need to walk into rooms looking for people who've successfully raised children, from whom you can learn something about being a good influence in your own children's lives. If you are married, look for married couples who can encourage and advise you in your marriage. Look for the best in the room and invite them to be part of your team. They may be busy, but I have learned that busy people are the ones who know how to get things done and make things work.

If there is a young boy or girl you admire for how their parents are raising them, invite them over to play with your kids and ask them how their parents discipline them, talk to them, delegate tasks. Invite their parents over and ask about their best practices and biggest regrets in their parenting journey. If you find someone at work who excels in an area of the business in which you would like to grow, ask them to mentor you or train you.

Always walk into a room looking to discover people you'd love to have join your team.

I remember one time when we needed a receptionist, and we weren't confident anyone in the church would fit the bill. But at my bank there was a head teller who was always so personable, welcoming, and accommodating. I saw that she always made people feel good when she interacted with them. I wanted someone like her to greet people when they came to the church during business hours. The next time I went to the bank, I couldn't resist asking if she would ever be interested in talking with me about a job. Long story short, I hired her and to this day she does excellent work for us.

You see, you must always look to discover people who can help you lead. I cannot be a pastor and lead a church if I'm sitting at the front desk answering phones. I need to find people who are gifted at greeting people and answering phones so I can pray, lead the staff, and prepare to preach on Sunday mornings. Empowering others to do work you don't need to be doing begins with finding godly, skilled people you can trust.

Another thing I've learned is that even while I'm looking for leaders to empower, I need to take time to develop those already entrusted to my care. Every week I take time to train, teach, develop, encourage, and challenge our staff. Good leadership is monkey see, monkey do. If I want my team to be the best version of themselves, I need to make sure they have access to me so they can learn from me. I take them with me on hospital visits and to funerals, celebrations, speaking engagements, and anything else I do. I want them to see in me what I expect from them. I invest time encouraging them to be the person God created them to be. I encourage them to understand that they don't have to be better than others on staff; I just want them to be the best they can be.

Part of developing others is training them to do a task 70 percent as well as you. After they become more skilled and experienced in that task, they will likely be able to do the task *better* than you. That's when your organization becomes better prepared for the next level of performance.

It's the same in parenting. You don't want your children to teach themselves how to do tasks around the home; you bring them beside you as you do the task. Then you allow them to do the task with your help. Eventually they can do the task alone; it may not be done perfectly, but with practice they get better. You wake up one day and they are doing the task on their own—and may have even found a better or more efficient way to do it.

Empowering those we lead and developing them is how we get more work done while giving others the gifts of personal growth and service to others. Micromanaging people does not build their self-confidence, and it keeps you from accomplishing all God has in store for you. Fortunately, the day came when I concluded that if I were going to accomplish more for God's glory, I needed to invest in others and trust them to do the job God has equipped them to do.

How do you empower others? You give them an assignment and show them an example of your expectation.

Give clear instructions and make sure you communicate how long the assignment should take. Once you give them the assignment, you give them authority to be able to fulfill the assignment. Let them do the task while you're available to answer questions. As the teammate or family member works on their assignment, you keep them accountable through regular touch bases where you can stay apprised and gently guide them to accomplish the task successfully.

Once they have done the job, affirm them in what they've done well. Remember, empowering others is about freeing yourself up to do the things only you can do. Give people room to make mistakes and do things differently than you. The goal is to accomplish a task, build unity as a team, encourage those you work with, and work toward a shared vision.

> **EMPOWERING OTHERS IS AN INVESTMENT IN THE LONG-TERM SUCCESS OF YOUR ENTERPRISE.**

Empowering others can be time-consuming on the front end, but it is an investment in the long-term success of your enterprise.

You cannot hold something tight in your grip and expect God to give you anything better. If Nehemiah had micromanaged the rebuilding of Jerusalem's wall, it may never have been completed. But the huge project took just fifty-two days to accomplish because Nehemiah delegated and empowered others to do what God had gifted them to do. He was able to stay focused on the vision God had given him and lead his team through various challenges along the way.

Yes, you can empower others—and realize that it gives you more capacity to do the things only you can do.

## FOR REFLECTION

1. Since God has called us to live and work among others, what tasks are you doing today that someone else could be doing?

2. How do you know when it is time to find more people to add to your team? How will you find them?

3. When empowering others, we should want them to succeed. What potential obstacles can you minimize for them? Have you clearly defined their roles? What will success look like for their task?

4. What character qualities will you look for in someone to whom you could give more responsibility?

5. Do you have regular touch bases scheduled with those whom you have tasked for a special role or assignment?

## PRINCIPLES TO REMEMBER

- Be highly selective in those you choose to help you.
- Clearly define the roles and responsibilities you are entrusting to them.
- Give those you select the authority and tools needed to do their jobs successfully.
- Express confidence in those you've entrusted. Thank and affirm them as they show progress and growth.
- Empower others by showing them how to do the job. Then let them do the job while you are there to coach and correct. Once they become more adept at the task, trust them to do it on their own.

## CHAPTER 13

# YES, YOU CAN LEAD BY BEING PRESENT

I SHARED EARLIER ABOUT playing baseball as a child and the opposing coach telling me I made a good play. One thing I didn't mention is that my family rarely came to watch me play. My coach would pick me up and take me home.

But one day, my stepfather came. I don't know why he chose that game or why he came at all. He often called me illegitimate and ignorant, and I knew he didn't like me very much. Do you want to know the power of presence? My stepfather, who often told me how worthless I was, came to watch me play baseball. Today, at age sixty, I still remember details from that game. I played for Boyd Nursery, and that night we were playing McMinnville TV Cable. I went three-for-four at bat. I hit a triple, and I knocked the cover off that ball. Just my stepfather showing up at the game encouraged me to step up and play the best game I ever played. His presence mattered.

In 2 Timothy 1:17 we see how one man's presence mattered for the apostle Paul. Paul wrote, "But when he [Onesiphorus] arrived in Rome he searched for me earnestly and found me." Paul was in prison, uncertain whether he'd be freed or martyred, and Onesiphorus came to Rome, searched and located Paul, and visited his friend. Onesiphorus never let *where* Paul was keep him from *who* Paul was. Paul was alone, and we are not created to be alone.

Paul wrote in verse 15, "You are aware that all who are in Asia turned away from me." This had to be hurtful to the apostle. He must have felt especially lonely. But Onesiphorus was a true friend. He was walking in when everyone else was walking out. Paul was deeply comforted by this unselfish act and able to rejoice that a faithful friend had come to spend time with him.

Being present is just being there and letting the person know he or she matters to you. Being present is just listening and not feeling that you must respond or fix the problem. Being present means walking in when everyone else is walking out.

Have you ever been in a place of loneliness and someone just showed up to be with you? There is no greater feeling than having company when you feel down and alone.

**BEING PRESENT MEANS WALKING IN WHEN EVERYONE ELSE IS WALKING OUT.**

If you are a spouse, don't underestimate the power of presence in your marriage. If you are a parent, never underestimate the power of your presence in your child's life. If you are an employee, don't underestimate the power of being present with your colleagues or your boss. If you are a CEO, owner of a company, or a boss in any way, don't underestimate the power of your presence among those who work for you. Your friendly presence will give those you lead confidence, assurance, pride, and a sense of importance. Your presence will give your people a sense of "team"—that they're not in it all by themselves. It will help them believe that "We can do anything together!" And when you truly care about those you influence, your presence can open their hearts for Jesus.

Your presence matters!

Once *The Jim Bakker Show* invited me to visit. This man had gone through a very public falling away from God and made poor choices that landed him in prison. He authored a book about what he did, confessing his failures and apologizing to the people he wronged. Previously, I'd heard him share one reason he was still in ministry.

Bakker said his job in prison was cleaning commodes. He felt abandoned by the church and everyone he had worked with. One day a guard told him he had a visitor, and he couldn't believe anyone had shown up to visit him. Plus, it was not a visitation day.

He went to see who had come to visit him, and it was Billy Graham.

"When I walked in, all I could see is this six-foot-something man, and I'm a five-foot-something guy," Bakker said. "And I walked in—he threw his arms around me, and he held me, and he said, 'Jim, I love you.' How could anybody love me looking like that? I had been disgraced to the world....And here he is in my prison holding me in his arms, telling me that he loved me."[1]

Bakker later said that Graham's just being there gave him incredible comfort. Here was a great man of God who had nothing to gain and everything to lose by associating with Bakker. But he came.

Bakker's story reminds me of Galatians 6:1: "Brothers, if anyone is caught in any transgression, you who are spiritual should restore him in a spirit of gentleness. Keep watch on yourself, lest you too be tempted."

I believe the greatest gift you can give someone is your presence. When you give people your time, energy, and love, you give them something they can never repay. And it can make all the difference.

## FOR REFLECTION

1. How are you currently showing your family or team that you are present for them?

2. What will you begin doing to be more present in the lives of those you lead?

3. What are things you can give up doing so you can be more present for the moments that matter?

4. What does Billy Graham's example say to you?

5. Is there someone you can think of who could use your presence right now? What is God leading you to do?

## PRINCIPLES TO REMEMBER

- Being present is being there for others, no matter their circumstances.

- Being present doesn't necessarily require you to say something or try to fix the problem. Often, your quiet presence is the best comfort.

- Your presence as a leader gives those you lead confidence, assurance, pride, and a sense of importance.

- Your presence enables your family or team to believe that "We can accomplish anything together!"

## CHAPTER 14

# YES, YOU CAN CHANGE

When I was growing up, I stayed with a couple named Roscoe and Thelma Coppinger in Tarlton, Tennessee. It was a rural area, as backwoods as you can get. They bathed me in a tub outside. When I wanted something to drink, they told me to get water out of the pan. I would walk over to the pan and inside that pan was a dipper. I would grab the dipper, get a drink, and put the dipper back into the pan. I never fathomed back then that one day we would be paying for bottled water. Water was timeless, but I am so glad that the method of drinking water has changed for me.

**IN LEADERSHIP THE PRINCIPLES ARE TIMELESS, BUT THE METHODS ARE EVER-CHANGING.**

Likewise, in leadership the principles are timeless, but the methods are ever-changing.

I can think of a company with a strong brand name that doesn't exist anymore. At one time, Blockbuster Video employed about 84,000 people and was a household name. If you've never heard of this company, you are much younger than I am. What happened? It no longer exists because it failed to change with the culture and transition to the digital age.

As I write this, our church is going through a tremendous change. When I looked at everything that needed to get done, I had a choice. I could keep Rock Springs right where we've been, or I could embrace change and begin leading our team into some needed transitions.

How do I transition my team toward a big change without compromising my principles? I look at the greatest leader to ever walk on the face of the earth: Jesus. There has never been, nor will there ever be, a better leader. He was a transitional leader in a position that was always changing. Jesus did not have a home during His ministry. He was constantly on the move and speaking with different people. He would be on His way to heal one person and someone else would stop Him in His tracks. He would go away to pray, and the crowds would follow Him. We have about fifty-two days of recorded life of Jesus, and of the fifty-two days, not one was like another day. As a leader, Jesus was an outstanding example of how to lead a team through major change.

One of my favorite things Jesus did as He led others through transition was that He spoke positively about the future. People facing change often dwell on what can go wrong. Jesus taught us to look at what is good. When preparing His disciples for His death, burial, and resurrection, He told them, "Truly, truly, I say to you, whoever believes in me will also do the works that I do; and greater works than these will he do, because I am going to the Father" (John 14:12). Jesus told His disciples that they would do even greater works after He was gone—that their best days were ahead of them. Jesus wanted His followers to know, and He wants us to know, that when we are in a season of change, there are better days ahead!

In our family life, our work, our ministries, our friendships, there are always changes. We need to embrace the necessary transitions, even if they are painful for a time. There is no change without resistance and a sense of loss. There is little growth without pain. But when we are willing to change, we inspire others to change.

I changed drastically by becoming a Christian. Here I was, from a dysfunctional family and a hard background, and still I gave my life to Jesus Christ. What inspired me to want to know Jesus? My mom. What was the change I saw in my mom? I saw Christ's transformation in her, and I saw how different her new lifestyle was. We don't have a problem with Christ changing people. We love 2 Corinthians 5:17, which promises, "Therefore, if anyone is in Christ, he is a new creation. The old has passed away; behold, the new has come." We are all for change when it comes to becoming Christ followers. And we believe it will all end with a huge change. To paraphrase 1 Thessalonians 4:16–17, the trumpet's going to toot and we're all going to scoot. Jesus is coming back for us. Now *that's* a change we can all embrace!

**WHEN WE ARE WILLING TO CHANGE, WE INSPIRE OTHERS TO CHANGE.**

But there are times when we refuse to change in our personal or professional lives. If, as a leader, you can look back and see no evidence of change over time, you're in trouble. Again, I'm not talking about disregarding your principles. I'm talking about how to accomplish what God has given you to do. Jesus called us to make disciples. That is the principle. But *how* to best make disciples—our methodology—may be different among individuals, families, or church members. Worldviews, communication methods, and how people process messages all change over time, and so must we. In order to grow and stay relevant, we must be open to change.

Sometimes we need to change because it is best for those we serve and care for. One of the first meetings I held at Rock Springs Church was to decide whether to lock the church at night. Some members felt we should keep the church open for those who wanted to come and pray day or night. Back then, we trusted everybody. But now culture has changed to become more dangerous, so we had to change. Today we have cameras and a full-time security team, and we lock up at night. What a change! Our principles haven't changed—we still pray, worship, and have biblical teaching each week. But we can no longer leave the building open 24/7 or go without security. We need to protect our people and their facility. Because culture has changed, we needed to change our methods.

**CHANGE IS NEEDED WHEN OLD METHODS ARE NO LONGER PRUDENT OR EFFECTIVE.**

Change is needed when old methods are no longer prudent or effective. In my early days at Rock Springs, we held morning and evening services on Sundays. Every service was full. That went on for years, and I didn't do anything to change. One Sunday night, we were using hymnals, and we were singing, "When we all get to heaven, what a day of rejoicing that will be!" I looked out at my teenage daughter, and I thought, "She wants to graduate high school, go to college, get married, have children, and work with special-needs kids, and here we are singing how great it will be when we all get to heaven." I prayed, "God, I am losing her." I sensed the Lord telling me, "Yeah, you are, and you're losing thousands of other teens along with her because you refuse to change." That's when I started campaigning to develop our worship to be more appealing to younger people.

As you might imagine, such a change upset some people in our congregation. This was painful for me. I decided that even though the transition might be painful and not everyone would agree with me, it was in the best interest of the church and would be worth the pain. We did transition, and indeed some tears were shed, but today those changes are complete, and the result has been wonderful.

How do you know if it's time to change methods, attitudes, or actions? If you are married, take a moment to check in with your spouse to see how he or she is doing and how they feel your relationship is working. Some methods may need to change in order to continue growing in your marriage.

If you parent middle schoolers and you still do things for them that you did when they were toddlers, you need to change. Middle school children can now do more for themselves than when they were younger. You still need to continue training up your child (principle), but your methods may need updating.

If you're at work doing the same thing you've always done but haven't received a promotion or raise, you may need to change something. You'll still come to work as you always have, but your work ethic, habits, and team spirit may need to change. If you want to lose weight and get healthy, you may need to change your diet and be more active every day. None of these things are easy. But to lead well, we must be open to improving ourselves as well as our enterprise, and that means we need to embrace change.

Culture will often tell you where you need to consider change. We can have all kinds of strategies to grow our families, teams, businesses, or organizations, but the culture will eat strategy for lunch. I always try to remember that the culture is paramount. I used to stand up in the pulpit and tell the congregation that we were going to have Sunday night service even though it was Super Bowl Sunday. Sunday morning, I would say, "We will be having service tonight, and I'd rather be in the Super Service than watching the Super Bowl!" And the congregation would dutifully shout, "Amen!" But then that night I always found myself preaching to an empty auditorium. I learned that culture eats strategy for lunch. When a leader is not conscientious of the culture, he's in trouble.

Sometimes change happens when you're not even looking. I call this an "eruption." An eruption is when something unexpected happens beyond your control and you can no longer do things the way you always have. One of the most memorable eruptions I remember as a pastor was COVID-19. Just before March 15, 2020, when our regular Sunday church activities were to take place, we were notified that it was against the law to meet corporately because of a virus that was shutting the world down. That was an eruption. No one knew or understood what was going on. Up till then, between 85 and 90 percent of our income came in via the offering plates when our congregation was sitting in service. Now, I didn't know what we'd do for income. That too was an eruption.

On Sunday, March 22, 2020, I drove to the church and the parking lot was empty. I walked into our church office and my team was waiting for me. They were nervous about what was going to happen, and honestly, I was too.

As their leader, I knew I needed to look fear in the face, so I said, "We are going to get through this." That is when we decided that if we could not meet as a church corporately, we were going to go into our people's homes online on Sundays and Wednesdays. On Thursdays, we would have live worship online. We decided that if the congregation could not come to our building, we could go stand in their yards and pray with them. The eruptions forced us to change how we had been doing church for more than thirty years.

Want to know what happened? Our church grew during COVID, and our offerings increased, and our online ministry grew, and we developed a monthly evangelism emphasis, and we began fostering churches. By embracing change, we were able to extend hope. When we did not know what to do, we asked the Lord for wisdom and kept our eyes on Him. We learned that when we are open to change, God can do wonders amid eruptions!

**GOD CAN DO WONDERS AMID ERUPTIONS!**

Successful leaders constantly have to adapt to change. They're willing to endure some procedural pain to achieve what is best for those they love and care for. If Jesus led so effectively through change, we can confidently follow His example. Embracing change will enable and empower those we influence to accomplish great things for God's glory.

Yes, you can embrace change!

## FOR REFLECTION

1. How does the prospect of change make you feel? Scared? Excited? Anxious? Energized? Why do you feel that way?

2. Is God nudging you to make a significant change in your family or workplace? What is He saying to you?

3. What specific things will you do to guide your people through the transitions needed to bring about the desired change?

4. Have you had a recent "eruption" in your life that is forcing change? How can you embrace the eruption? What creative ways can you think of to transition what you were doing to what you need to be doing now?

## PRINCIPLES TO REMEMBER

- In leadership, the principles are timeless, but the methods are ever-changing.
- There is no change without resistance and loss.
- When we embrace change, we inspire others to change.
- Change is needed when the current methods are no longer prudent or effective.
- Eruptions invite and inspire change. Embrace and grow from them!

# PART V

# LEADING WHEN LIFE IS HARD

*I have learned to kiss the waves that throw me up against the Rock of Ages.*
—C. H. Spurgeon

## CHAPTER 15

# YES, YOU CAN LEAD WHEN LIFE IS HARD

Years ago, when we were young, Barbara and I were certified to be foster parents. We had already adopted our precious daughter, Savannah Abigail, and we had the opportunity to bring another baby girl into our home and hearts. We were so excited!

Barbara and I loved that little girl. We could not have children naturally, and we loved having children in our home. One day we got the call from the Division of Family and Children Services (DFCS), and they told us that we were going to be able to adopt this little girl we had grown to love so much. We were thrilled.

But later I was on the phone with DFCS, and they said, "Mr. Tate, we need to make you aware of something. We are looking at reunification between this little girl and her biological parents."

I said, "No, no. Remember, you said we would be able to adopt her."

"Well, that has changed, Mr. Tate. We will need the baby ready to be returned to her parents in a month." I told them I would not create any more hurt on my wife and our little girl, Savannah, by keeping the baby another month. I went home and told Barbara. I asked her to take Savannah and leave so I could clean out that sweet baby's room so there would not be any reminders of her after I returned her to DFCS.

That very same night was our church's VBS finale, and I needed to be there to close out the week. I got up and welcomed everyone. I said that it had been a wonderful week at VBS, and everyone had done a wonderful job. I put on a big smile, got through the evening, and went home. I was a young kid at the time, but I learned a big lesson: Sometimes leaders must minister and lend hope even when they are hurting.

Jesus taught us this in Matthew 14. His cousin John the Baptist had been beheaded, and Jesus' disciples came to deliver the news to Him. "Now when Jesus heard this, he withdrew from there in a boat to a desolate place by himself. But when the crowds heard it, they followed him on foot from the towns. When he went ashore, he saw a great crowd, and he had compassion on them and healed their sick" (vv. 13–14). After this, the disciples asked the Lord to send the multitudes away to go eat. Jesus told them, "They need not go away; you give them something to eat" (v. 16). Jesus had withdrawn from the crowd to grieve, but He ended up serving the crowd and feeding them. Leading others is hard, especially when you're hurting. Jesus shows us that you cannot bring your hurt with you; you must bring hope.

**SOMETIMES LEADERS MUST MINISTER AND LEND HOPE EVEN WHEN THEY ARE HURTING.**

What these hard lessons in life have taught me is that I need to have emotional maturity when tough times come. I've learned that I need to be bigger than my emotions. I remember one time I received news that hit me hard, and it was personal. It seemed someone was stirring up a potential conflict with me. I had to be somewhere in less than thirty minutes after hearing this news that almost shattered me. I wanted to stay home and not go anywhere, but I had a commitment that I could not delegate. To do what I needed to do next, I had to get my mind collected and put on hold the disheartening news I had just been told.

In that moment, I had to be bigger than my emotions.

After I got home, I was able to deal with the news that had been so hard earlier that day. When you don't have emotional maturity, it can manifest itself in conflict with others and cause significant damage. When disagreements arise, you as a leader need to decide that you are not going to make an enemy out of a person because they disagree with you. You must decide to care for the relationship and temporarily walk away until the emotion subsides.

Let me give you an example of what I mean. John Wesley and George Whitefield were both church leaders. Wesley was an Arminian, and Whitefield more of a Puritan in thought within the Methodist religion. They were in great conflict over what they believed. One day someone asked Whitefield if he expected to see John Wesley in heaven. Whitefield responded, "I fear not, for he will be so near the eternal throne and we at such a distance, we shall hardly get sight of him."[1] Whitefield knew what emotional maturity was. He was able to see through the doctrinal conflict and remember that even though he disagreed with Wesley, Wesley was a child of God.

We should aspire to be like that when we disagree with others. We must realize that in any conflict, we choose to pick up either a can of gas or a can of water. When we pick up a gas can, we're choosing to add fuel to the flame. But if we choose water, we're choosing to cool the argument down. In marriage you get to choose which can you pick up in the middle of intense interaction. If you disagree with someone at work, you choose the can you'll pick up. If you are online and disagree with someone's post, you choose. Those who are emotionally immature pour gas on the fire. Good leaders pour water on a crisis and cool things down. They keep their heads when everyone else is losing theirs.

If you want to lead effectively through conflict, you must have emotional maturity.

I have also learned that when I'm going through something hard, I need to be persistent in the things I know God has called me to. Persistence is what got the snail on the ark, and it is what separates good leaders from those who only dream of leading. One time we had a yard with an oak tree in it. One day after a good rain I walked outside and noticed that mushrooms had popped up all over the yard. I looked at the mushrooms and quickly began kicking them over. I stopped for a moment and gazed up at the oak tree, thinking that it would take a lot more than me kicking that tree to knock it over. Then I looked back down at the mushrooms and thought, "That oak tree is just a nut that refused to quit."

**AN OAK TREE IS JUST A NUT THAT REFUSED TO QUIT.**

I don't want to be a mushroom leader; I want to be an oak tree leader. It takes persistence to do that. Sometimes when life gets hard and I'm tempted to quit, I think about the persistence of John Wesley. People have created a popular retelling, based on incidents from his real life, that paints a picture of what his ministry was often like:

**Sunday, a.m., May 5**
Preached in St. Ann's. Was asked not to come back anymore.

**Sunday p.m., May 5**
Preached in St. John's. Deacons said, "Get out and stay out."

**Sunday, a.m., May 12**
Preached in St. Jude's. Cannot go back there either.

**Sunday, a.m., May 19**
Preached in St. Somebody Else's. Deacons called special meeting and said I couldn't return.

**Sunday, p.m., May 19**
Preached on the street. Kicked off the street.

**Sunday, a.m., May 26**
Preached in meadow, chased out of meadow as bull was turned loose during service.

**Sunday, a.m., June 2**
Preached out at the edge of town, kicked off the highway.

**Sunday, p.m., June 2**
Afternoon service. Preached in a pasture, 10,000 people came out to hear me.[2]

Now this isn't exactly what is written in Wesley's journal, but it does give you an idea of the opposition he often faced. Wesley endured some tough seasons—but the Lord honored his perseverance and did a mighty work through him! Thinking about what Wesley went through motivates me to be persistent and drives me right back to what God has called me to do.

I have also found that when you're leading, you are often bleeding. There is a story in the Bible that always encourages me when I face huge obstacles. Joshua 1:1–3 tells us, "After the death of Moses the servant of the LORD, the LORD said to Joshua the son of Nun, Moses' assistant, 'Moses my servant is dead. Now therefore arise, go over this Jordan, you and all this people, into the land that I am giving to them, to the people of Israel. Every place that the sole of your foot will tread upon I have given to you, just as I promised to Moses.'"

At this moment in Israel's long journey, there were at least three obstacles impeding them from crossing into the Promised Land. First, Moses had died. He had been their leader for more than forty years. Moses had been the one God spoke to. Moses received the Law from the Lord. Moses was the mediator between Israel and God. Then Moses died, and now Joshua was in charge. The Scriptures tell us that Moses had trained Joshua for the job—but leadership changes can be tough.

The second obstacle was that the river was at flood stage. Israel would be crossing the Jordan in springtime, when snow melted down from Mount Lebanon into the river. There were also abundant spring rains. This was a new generation of Israel, raised in the wilderness. These people did not experience the Red Sea parting. It would have been frightening for them to see these rushing waters.

And there was a third obstacle. Deuteronomy 7:1 says as soon as Israel crossed the Jordan, they would face seven hostile nations mightier than they were. As a leader, in any environment, you will face obstacles.

Is there something you want to accomplish? Remember, everything worthwhile that you'd like to accomplish is uphill. Paul Harvey said, "You can always tell when you are on the road to success; it's uphill all the way."[3]

Anywhere there is motion, there is friction. Anywhere there is opportunity, there is opposition.

But you cannot have uphill hopes with downhill habits. The idea that knowing something must be from God because it is easy or smooth is not biblical. The nation of Israel was promised the land by God, but nothing about gaining the land was easy. As their new leader, Joshua encouraged the people. He gave them responsibility. He sought the Lord for wisdom and guidance. He led with courage and faced his obstacles. One by one he faced them. Israel crossed the Jordan. They conquered Jericho.

> **WESLEY HAD HAD A TOUGH MAY—BUT THE LORD HONORED HIS PERSEVERANCE AND DID A MIGHTY WORK THROUGH HIM ON JUNE 2!**

The nation of Israel was going into the land of milk and honey, but they would encounter "stings and stuff." If you're going to get honey, you will get stings. If you're going to get milk, you're going to step in "stuff."

You are never *not* going to have problems. I have experienced things that were surely of God, but they were still difficult. Pastoring Rock Springs Church has not been easy. There is never a day without a difficulty. But uphill challenges just go with leadership. Vance Havner said, "A preacher should have the mind of a scholar, the heart of a child, and the hide of a rhinoceros. His biggest problem is how to toughen his hide without hardening his heart."[4] This is not only true for pastors, but true for anyone leading. Real leaders are not always the most popular, because they have to deal with the uphills.

You will encounter obstacles, and sometimes you may just run out of gas. This is the time for you to lean into the Lord and know that you are experiencing an opportunity to grow in your faith. How can you grow through these obstacles?

1. Admit that you are in a season of discouragement.

2. Ask God to restore your passion. Psalm 51:12 says, "Restore to me the joy of your salvation, and uphold me with a willing spirit."

3. Recommit to serving. You need to serve others to heal. Your sense of significance and purpose will regenerate as you serve others.

Expect obstacles and uphill challenges and ask the Lord to strengthen and guide you to power through them. When I look back over what God has done in my life, I see that growth takes place in the valley. He promises to walk us *through* the valley, not around it. If we keep our eyes on Him through the valley, we will grow into stronger, wiser leaders. Growth takes place in the valley.

I trust the Lord more today because of yesterday's valleys. I've experienced a relationship with Him that I would not have experienced without the challenging times. I've seen that each hard circumstance was worth it on the other side. Through tough times, I have met people who have loved, supported, encouraged, and challenged me to grow as a person, husband, dad, pastor, and friend.

As leaders, we must always keep in mind that we are dealers in hope. When life is hard, ministry is hard, marriage is hard, or finances are hard, it is our job to model humility, persistence, stability, courage, and confidence among those we lead.

Yes, you can lead when life is hard!

## FOR REFLECTION

1. How have you typically responded when life is hard?
2. How can you lend hope to others when you are hurting?
3. There are two kinds of people in a conflict: One is a gas can, the other is a water can. Which one do you tend to be? If you are a gas can, how can you become a water can?
4. How do you know you are doing what God has called you to do? What are things you can do to remember your calling when life gets challenging?
5. How are you facing the obstacles that are in your way today? What have you learned in this chapter that will help you handle hurts and obstacles in the future?

## PRINCIPLES TO REMEMBER

- When life is hard, you can lend hope to others who are hurting.
- In conflict, you must be bigger than your emotions.
- You are never going to *not* have problems. Lean into the Lord and know that you are experiencing an opportunity to grow in your faith.
- God promises to walk us *through* the valley, not around it. Growth takes place in the valley.

CHAPTER 16

# YES, YOU CAN RECOVER FROM DISCOURAGEMENT

IN MY YEARS as a pastor, I have occasionally received texts or anonymous letters that were not kind. I would read them, feel hurt and defensive, and my spirit would plummet. As a young pastor, I did not manage discouragement very well.

As I've grown older, I try to look at the information I receive and pray, "Lord, there is a lot of smoke here. Is there a little fire?" I now choose to examine the discouraging words and ask what I can learn from them. So if I were to receive a message with six discouraging assertions, I try to ask myself, "Is there any truth in this?" Rarely will all hurtful words be true, but I look for what truth could be there. This enables me to move past any hurt and learn something instead of allowing discouragement to ruin my day, week, or month.

**THE WORD OF GOD DEFEATS DISCOURAGEMENT.**

You cannot let people who hurt you determine your outlook or actions. You don't want to become bitter; you want to become better. When I have felt myself descending into hurt and discouragement, I've found that God's Word lifts my spirit and gives me wisdom and strength. The Word of God defeats discouragement.

I believe Jeremiah 29:11: "'For I know the plans I have for you,' declares the LORD, 'plans to prosper you, and not harm you, plans to give you a hope and a future'" (NIV). And Romans 8:28 has been another go-to verse: "And we know that for those who love God all things work together for good, for those who are called according to his purpose."

One of my favorite Bible stories also helps me rise above discouragement. In Genesis 29, Isaac's younger son, Jacob, left his family in fear after he stole his brother's blessing. Jacob encountered a man named Laban, who was even more of a trickster than Jacob. Laban had at least two daughters. One was Rachel, who "was beautiful in form and appearance." The other was Leah, whose "eyes were weak."

It didn't take long for Rachel to catch Jacob's eye. He made a deal with Rachel's dad: If Jacob served seven years on Laban's ranch, Laban would give him Rachel in marriage. The account reads, "So Jacob served seven years for Rachel, and they seemed to him but a few days because of the love he had for her" (v. 20). Finally the wedding night arrived, but the devious Laban hid his older daughter Leah behind the veil. Unsuspectingly, Jacob married Leah instead of Rachel.

As I review this story, of course I feel for Jacob. But then another thought occurs to me: Imagine being Leah! She wasn't the one Jacob wanted. On the wedding night, when it was dark, Jacob took Leah to bed thinking she was Rachel. The next morning, once he realized he'd been duped, he was terribly upset. Jacob had wanted beautiful Rachel, and he'd worked seven years to marry her. Jacob was stuck, and so was Leah.

His sneaky father-in-law, Laban, then told Jacob he could work seven more years for Rachel. So Jacob began another seven years' labor in order to marry Rachel. While he didn't love Leah, he was a dutiful husband, and they had a child named Reuben. Leah said, "Now my husband will love me" (v.32). Guess what? Jacob still didn't love Leah. They had another son and named him Simeon. Leah said, "Because the LORD has heard that I am hated, he has given me this son also" (v. 33). Jacob and Leah had a third son, Levi. And Leah said, "Now this time my husband will be attached to me, because I have borne him three sons" (v. 34). Still, Jacob did not love her.

And Leah knew she was unloved. Talk about discouragement! But when she bore a fourth son, she shifted her outlook. "This time I will praise the LORD," Leah said (v. 35). She didn't hope that maybe this time Jacob would love her. She determined to just praise the Lord. She had learned that her relationship with Jacob was not the most important thing; her relationship with the Lord was what really mattered.

You see, we are going to have times of discouragement. And what we must decide is that we're going to praise the Lord.

You may be saying, "Benny, you said God works all things together for good. What is so good about this story?" Well, let's see what became of each of Leah's sons. The third son, Levi, became the tribe of Levi, which means that Moses came from her. Jacob did not love her and yet the Levitical priesthood came from her. Her fourth son was Judah, which means "praise." Judah's offspring became King David. In Revelation 5:5, John writes of Jesus Christ, born of the "tribe of Judah, the Root of David." Jesus came from Leah's lineage! God used an unlikely, plain, unloved woman to pave the way for Jesus to enter our world!

You know what my foundation is? Not losing faith when things don't turn out the way I want. What I know is that God has a plan. He has a plan when we cannot see it. He has a plan when we don't understand it. He doesn't owe us explanations. We live our lives on God's promises. Like Leah, we decide to trust Him.

As leaders, we need to know how to recover from discouragement. I have found that the best way is to find the positive in the negative. I call it "flipping the script."

In baseball, if your batting average is .300, you're reaching base only three out of every ten at-bats, only 30 percent of the time. You could become discouraged and consider yourself a failure. But batting .300 in baseball is success! It might get you into the Hall of Fame! It's all in how you look at the information. Flip the script! Babe Ruth struck out 1,330 times (that was a record). He also hit 714 home runs! We must keep swinging when life is discouraging. There are times you will get discouraged, but look for the positives and focus on what's good in the situation. Love and trust God to show you clearly what He wants you to learn.

**THE BEST WAY TO RECOVER FROM DISCOURAGEMENT IS TO FLIP THE SCRIPT.**

Look at how Jesus cared for Peter when Peter was discouraged. After Jesus had been resurrected, Peter was still ashamed at how he had denied Jesus three times. In John 21, Jesus said to him, "Peter, if you love Me, tend my sheep." Often, we get discouraged because of people. Jesus told Peter, and He tells us, "Love Me and serve the people."

When we are discouraged, we are to love and trust God and tend those He's placed in our care. He will change our perspective and bring us out of our despair.

Yes, you can recover from discouragement!

## FOR REFLECTION

1. Think back to a time when someone said discouraging words to you. How did you deal with it? Was there any truth to what was said? If so, how did you use the little truth to become better?

2. When you think about needing encouragement, what scriptures come to mind? How would it strengthen you if you were to memorize a few of those promises?

3. Next time you find yourself discouraged, what action will you take to "flip the script"?

4. What other thoughts caught your attention in this chapter that you'd like to keep in mind for the future?

## PRINCIPLES TO REMEMBER

- When you're disheartened by hurtful words, find the truth in the person's words and ask God to help you grow from it.

- When you're discouraged, turn to the Word of God first.

- Flip the script—find and focus on the positive in the situation.

- As Jesus told Peter when the disciple was discouraged, love God and care more deeply for those He puts in front of you.

CHAPTER 17

# YES, YOU CAN OVERCOME INSECURITY

I HAVE STRUGGLED WITH insecurity most of my life.

As children, my siblings and I left home with our mother nearly twenty times. Sometimes we would leave in the middle of the night and be gone for weeks. Eventually we would go back, and the situation would be the same—more abuse. I was told repeatedly that I would not amount to anything. Due to bad circumstances and poor choices, I was also homeless for parts of my life. And I must confess, the insecurity I developed back then has bled over into my relationships at home and at work.

We all have some degree of insecurity. We have all been made fun of, endured tough situations, made bad decisions, or lived with something we don't like about ourselves. As leaders, we need to know how to overcome insecurity as we lead and care for those God has given us to influence.

Let's look again at Peter, this time before Jesus was arrested. Jesus was with His disciples at the Passover dinner in the Upper Room. Matthew 26 tells us, "Then Jesus said to them, *You will all fall away because of me this night.* For it is written, 'I will strike the shepherd, and the sheep of the flock shall be scattered'" (v. 31, emphasis added). But Peter, always the bold one, answered, "Though they all fall away because of you, I will never fall away" (v. 33). Peter was telling Jesus, if there is anyone you can count on, I'm your guy! But Jesus responded to Peter, "Truly, I tell you, this very night, before the rooster crows, you will deny me three times" (v. 34).

As we know, the denial happened just as Jesus said. If you are insecure right now because you feel you have disappointed the Lord, remember that He knew what you were going to do before you did it. He still loves and cares about you, just as He loved and cared for Peter.

What do you think went through Peter's mind when he heard the rooster crow? Had he disqualified himself as the rock, a name Jesus had given him? A leader among the Twelve, he'd gone from tough guy to coward in just a few short minutes, vehemently denying three times that he even knew the Man.

What a failure! The Bible tells us he left the scene and wept bitterly. Undoubtedly, Peter was deeply ashamed of his actions—even embarrassed. This had to have made him feel *very* insecure around his colleagues and, later, around Jesus Himself.

But as we saw in an earlier chapter, Jesus showed how He feels about us when we disappoint Him. He made sure Peter understood that he was forgiven and loved—and that he still had kingdom work to do. Jesus recommissioned the man who had failed Him and entrusted him with a vital mission: love and care for those for whom Jesus had died.

He enabled Peter to overcome his battered self-esteem and insecurity—and truly be the leader Christ anointed him to be.

Every single one of us has strengths and weaknesses. And like Peter, the best of us are still people. We all have some self-esteem issues—insecurities—from long ago or from recent happenings. But we cannot let these issues impede us from leading those the Lord has entrusted to us. We must overcome. And with God's help and strength, we can!

How? We must base our self-esteem in Christ. You are God's creation, made in His image. The best way to begin believing this for yourself is to be in your Bible. Read what God says about you! You are fearfully and wonderfully made (Psalm 139:14). You are *so* loved (John 3:16). You are a new creation in Christ (2 Corinthians 5:17). You are God's workmanship (Ephesians 2:10). You are created in His image (Genesis 1:27). When you can believe what God says about you, you're well on your way to overcoming insecurity in your life. Find your identity in Christ, not in your position or accomplishments.

**FIND YOUR IDENTITY IN CHRIST, NOT IN YOUR POSITION OR ACCOMPLISHMENTS.**

Another thing that has helped me rise above insecurity is brokenness. That's right, brokenness. Brokenness on earth creates openness in heaven. When we allow God to break us of self-sufficiency and self-importance, it creates security in our lives. Here's how it works: When I am broken, that is when I desperately need God. I have gone through seasons where God just broke me. A. W. Tozer wrote, "It is doubtful whether God can bless a man greatly until He has hurt him deeply."[1]

Through personal *brokenness*, God has developed *qualities* in me that He knew I needed. Qualities such as empathy and forgiveness. As I have gotten older, not only has my hair gotten gray, but things I was adamant about have gotten gray too. There are things in life that seem so important until you have been through a season of being broken. When you come out of that season, you have empathy you did not have before, and you realize that extending forgiveness is easier because you see others in a better light.

Seasons of brokenness have also caused me to become a better giver. When circumstances have broken me, I've learned to depend on others and trust people more. Brokenness has developed security in my life. God wanted me to know that anything good in my life is a gift from Him and that I am nothing apart from Him. Some of my best leadership principles have come from being broken.

Another way I found victory over insecurity was to learn to love people better—and let people love me. I remember the day this came to my attention. My doctor, who knew me and knew my story, asked, "When you embrace people, do you lead the embrace?"

**YOU MUST LEARN TO GIVE AND RECEIVE LOVE TOO! YOU DESERVE TO BE LOVED.**

I told him I did.

Then he put his hand on my back and asked, "You're uncomfortable with that, aren't you?"

"Yeah," I said.

"Do you know why you're uncomfortable with being touched?"

"No."

He said, "Because you don't feel you are worthy to be loved or that anyone would want to express love to you. Benny, you must learn to give love—but you also need to learn to receive love. You deserve being loved."

I want you to know that you must learn to give and receive love too! You deserve to be loved.

What else builds security? Be a lifelong learner. Hosea 4:6 says, "My people are destroyed for lack of knowledge." Knowledge breeds confidence and security in your life. Make a commitment to be a lifelong learner as you lead others. Don't be a know-it-all, be a learn-it-all! I'll offer some practical ways to continue learning in the next chapter.

If you don't deal with insecurity in your life, it will not only affect you but also those you influence. Your insecurity will become their insecurity. But God can help you overcome, if you let Him.

## FOR REFLECTION

1. In what areas in your life have you felt insecure?
2. Who is being impacted by your insecurity today? How is it affecting them?
3. Do you believe the things you are insecure about may disqualify you from being used by God? Why or why not?
4. Have you seen God use brokenness for your good?
5. What are you doing today to continue learning? What would you like to be doing?

## PRINCIPLES TO REMEMBER

- To overcome insecurity, you should find your identity in Jesus.
- Brokenness often helps a leader overcome insecurity because it helps you become more secure in your relationship with Christ.
- When you don't deal with your insecurities, those you lead feel insecure.
- Ask God and trust Him to help you overcome any lingering insecurity.

## PART VI

# INSPIRED TO LEAD? WHAT DO I DO NEXT?

*You will be the same person in five years as you are today except for the people you meet and the books you read.*
—Charlie "Tremendous" Jones

## CHAPTER 18

# YES, YOU CAN CONTINUE TO GROW

SOMETIMES WE NEED to ask ourselves, "Do I have thirty years of experience, or do I have one year of experience thirty times?"

It doesn't matter how long you've been doing something if you are not growing where you're planted. It is imperative that we leaders become a better version of ourselves with each passing day. If you are a stay-at-home mom, you should be asking yourself, "What am I doing today that will make me a better version of myself tomorrow?" If you're a mechanic, ask yourself, "What can I do today that will make me a better version of myself tomorrow?"

Anybody can ask themselves that question and find a good answer. You can read your Bible every day, which will make you a better version of yourself. You can go for regular walks or decide to stop a bad habit. Today, if you were to look in the bag that goes everywhere with me, you would find books, magazines, and articles; I'm always trying to grow and develop to be better. In my pocket, you'd find a Scripture card that I can pull out to memorize as I have a moment. You can decide to read two pages per day of a book on Christian growth or leadership. Start small and think tall.

I believe when you listen to a podcast, it will add value to your leadership. However, if you want to multiply your leadership, you need to get into a room with proven leaders and learn. Meet with leaders who are successful in the area in which you would like to grow; observe their personal discipline and ask what they do daily to get better.

**START SMALL AND THINK TALL.**

If you are a pastor, ask a pastor you admire how he has grown his church. Ask to visit and ask questions. If you are a spouse, find a couple who has been married a while, and ask if you could spend time with them. If you are an executive assistant and you want to serve your boss better, find another executive assistant who does an excellent job. Do you see what I mean? Try to get into the presence of someone who has been where you are and learn. Always look for opportunities to gain insights and advice that will help you continue to grow.

I want to remind you that when I was a young pastor, we didn't have extra money, and I certainly had not been trained as a pastor. So Barbara and I needed to save money for me to attend pastoral conferences. One time we saved up about forty-nine dollars to send me to my first conference. I will never forget it. The name of the conference was "154 Ways to Grow Your Sunday School." I knew if our church was ever going to grow, I needed to expose myself to other people and new ideas.

There were other things I did to grow myself as a pastor and leader. I would reach out to pastors of large churches. I would drive to them, be there when they asked me to arrive, bring my legal pad with prepared questions, and take notes. I was determined to grow personally and be a better version of myself for the sake of those I influenced. I want to always be teachable. Barbara is an excellent example to me. Every day, she is in her Bible and listening to good preachers and teachers on radio or TV. She is always studying and growing.

Ralph Waldo Emerson wrote, "In my walks, every man I meet is my superior in some way, and in that I learn from him."[1] Whoever you are as a leader, it's good to be reminded that your family or organization will not grow around you—it will grow under you. If you don't keep learning and growing, you will lose your edge—and maybe the respect of those who follow you.

No, growth is not easy. But it's mandatory for good leaders. Those you care for and have influence over are counting on you to grow.

Growth is hard. It can be painful. If we are going to lead with excellence and be used of God to our fullest, we must boldly face up to the discipline and pain of growth, so we are leading from our absolute best.

**THOSE YOU CARE FOR AND HAVE INFLUENCE OVER ARE COUNTING ON YOU TO GROW.**

When the pain is greater than you're willing to absorb, you may have reached the place in your leadership where growth will no longer happen. When it all becomes "too much" and you can't muster the energy to push through the pain of self-reflection, past hurts, current hurts, or any opportunity to heal and grow, that is where you stop growing. One year's experience repeated thirty times. Your marriage stops growing, your parenting stops growing, your relationships stop flourishing, your organization goes flat, or your church stops reaching others.

The result? Mediocrity.

Or, to put it more bluntly, slow death. Sad but true: If you're not growing, you're dying.

Years ago, I looked within my denomination and did not see growth in our leaders. Their leadership and vision were mediocre at best. I decided I had to do something different, and that meant I needed to do something uncomfortable. I needed to step outside my denomination in order to learn and develop myself and our church. I traveled to Phoenix to study two men—one a Lutheran and the other Assembly of God. These denominations are extreme opposites in some of their doctrine, but the men were both doing extreme works for God. I knew I could learn from them, and I did! Don't let your background or the way things have always been done be a barrier to your learning and growth. God may use other people, other viewpoints and ideas, or recent technology to grow you. Eat the blackberries and spit out the briars! You don't have to agree 100 percent with someone to learn from them. Open your mind to something new. The strength of your marriage, family, work, ministry, or organization lies in your willingness to listen and learn.

If you really want to grow and lead at the next level, the following are some ideas that have proven invaluable in my journey.

First, you need to become a good listener. Good leaders listen and learn from other successful leaders. They listen and learn from their peers. They listen and learn from those they lead. The Bible tells us in James 1:19, "Know this, my beloved brothers: let every person be quick to hear, slow to speak." There is a reason God gave us two ears and one mouth. You don't grow by talking; you grow by listening.

I am convinced that the older leaders get, the less they should speak. I spoke more as a younger man than I do as an older man. One thing I've learned is that we don't need to say everything we know and everything we feel. Sometimes we just need to be silent and listen and learn.

And this is true even when others are saying harsh or untrue things about us.

Remember how Jesus responded when He was being falsely accused? He remained silent. There will be times when we should not even attempt to defend ourselves. Not everyone needs to know why you made the parenting decision you made. Not everyone needs to understand why your family decided to stop doing what others were doing. Not every team member needs to know why upper management decided to change procedures. I do think you should be transparent and let your family and team know what they need to know, but if the information you have is hurtful, or if you need some time to process, or if an idea needs time to develop, they don't need to know today. As a leader, you may sometimes need to remember the quote from our friend Nehemiah: "I am doing a great work and I cannot come down" (6:3). Young leaders today share too much. They need to be quiet and listen. This was a mistake I made too often. At age twenty-five, I did not know enough to be saying as much as I was saying. If I could go back, I would concentrate more on listening and a whole lot less on talking. Larry King said, "I never learned anything when I was talking."[2] Leaders sometimes need to keep silent—and listen.

Another practice I encourage leaders to implement at work is remembering people's names. This is such a wonderful way to care for people. Of course, you won't need to work on memorizing people's names in your family (I hope), but when you encounter someone, try to greet them by name or use their name in conversation. It makes them feel that you value them. By using their name and asking what's going on in their life, you show that they are interesting to you and that you care.

There's another thing I do that helps me grow as a leader: I pick up my pen.

We are in the digital and social media age. We text, tweet, email, and post. But I will tell you that none of that is as powerful as picking up a pen and writing a note to someone. I have all kinds of friends who reach out to me monthly. Their names are Verizon, Central Georgia EMC, United Bank, and many others. When I get home, I look through the mail and see greetings from all those faithful friends. But if I see a handwritten card with my name on it, this is what I open first!

**PICK UP YOUR PEN.**

When did I learn the importance of picking up a pen to be a better leader? Thirty-five years ago. When we left our church in Tennessee to come to Georgia, there was a lady in our Tennessee church named Elizabeth Howell. We loved her deeply. We were kids at the time, and she took good care of us. When I told her we were moving to Georgia, she replied, "Barbara is going to have a tough time with you moving her away. Let me tell you what I'm going to do. Every week for your first year there, I am going to write you and Barbara a card and tell you what is going on around here. I will tell you a little bit about what is going on with me and in the county where we live, and I am going to ask about the both of you."

*Yes, You Can Continue to Grow*

For fifty-two weeks, Elizabeth Howell was true to her word. Every week we watched our mail and enjoyed her updates. We felt assured that she cared about us and was praying for our new ministry. She taught me the power of picking up my pen.

How will this help you grow as a leader? It will help set you apart from all the digital "noise" and show those you influence that you're thinking of them—that you care enough to sit down, pick up a card, write a note, find a stamp, address the card, and put it in the mailbox. I keep cards in my desk so when someone comes to mind, I can jot a quick note. When I hear that someone has experienced a loss, is facing a challenge, or has something to celebrate, I take a moment and pick up my pen.

When Paul was in a Roman prison, he wrote a letter to Philemon and had it sent more than thirteen hundred miles away. In this letter he teaches us how to write a letter. First, Paul made the letter personal. In Philemon, he wrote, "Grace to you and peace from God our Father and the Lord Jesus Christ. I thank my God *always when I remember you in my prayers*, because *I hear of your love and of the faith* that you have toward the Lord Jesus and for all the saints.... For *I have derived much joy and comfort from your love*, my brother, because the hearts of the saints have been refreshed through you" (vv. 3–5, 7, emphases added).

See how Paul made the letter personal? Then Paul wrote about the present. He said, "I hear" and "I have derived." He said that Philemon's work for the Lord made him proud. Then we read, "...because the hearts of the saints have been refreshed." Paul clearly defined the reason he was proud.

Can you think of a better model to follow? I think we've lost the art of handwriting cards and letters these days.

But you can rise above and beyond the "noise." Picking up a pen to bless someone with a thoughtful message of thanks, affirmation, or encouragement is a sign that you are growing as a leader.

Babe Ruth said, "Yesterday's home runs don't win today's games."[3] If we want to grow in our leadership, we cannot keep doing what we've always done. God is doing new things in our lives, and He wants to give us a new vision and a new direction. We need to face our challenges and embrace growth. Yes, you can grow!

## FOR REFLECTION

1. In your own words, why is it vital for leaders to continue to grow personally and professionally?
2. What practices do you try to do regularly to help you grow?
3. Think of some leaders you'd like to spend time with and learn from. What would you ask them? Why not make an appointment this week?
4. How do you typically react when you are in a painful spot as leader? What can you do to better handle the "pain" and grow through the experience?
5. What practices would you like to put to work this week?

## PRINCIPLES TO REMEMBER

- A leader should always strive to continue to grow.
- When deciding to grow, start small and think tall.
- Growth can be uncomfortable. Embrace the discomfort.
- If you want to grow your leadership ability, get together with successful leaders.
- Good leaders are good listeners.
- Good leaders make a point to remember people's names.
- Set yourself above and apart: Pick up a pen—often.

CHAPTER 19

# YES, YOU CAN BE GENEROUS

WHEN I WAS a young pastor, there wasn't much I could do financially for people. Barbara and I lived in a furnished trailer (because we did not own any furniture), and we were barely able to make ends meet. We could not afford to take people out to eat, so we would invite them over. I learned early on that generosity is an issue of the heart. Today, I wake up every day and ask myself, "Who can I give to today?"

A good leader leads in every aspect of life. We should lead in generosity, service, example, and attitude. When I look at 1 Chronicles 29, I see how King David led the way in generosity to the building campaign for the temple: "Moreover, in addition to all that I have provided for the holy house, I have a treasure of my own of gold and silver, and because of my devotion to the house of my God I give it to the house of my God" (v. 3). As a result of David's example, others followed. "Then the leaders of fathers' houses made their freewill offerings, as did also the leaders of the tribes, the commanders of thousands and of hundreds, and the officers over the king's work" (v. 6). Leadership is monkey see, monkey do.

Generosity is not an area of leadership that most people talk about. Do you know the Scriptures talk about prayer

371 times? And the word *love* 714 times. The ideas of generosity, giving, or money are cited 2,152 times. Why does God say so much about money? Because money says so much about you and your heart. Generous people always have more than enough, and takers never have enough. I believe that when God blesses us, He has more than us in mind. It is more blessed to be generous than to see what we can take.

During the pandemic when our congregation could not meet at church, I told Barbara that we had to do something to express our personal seeds of faith. The Lord led me to increase our giving. We didn't know what our income was going to be or how it would be affected. Barbara has always been so supportive, yet she asked, "Why do you say that?" I told her, "God is our source, Barbara." What we'd learned was that we don't live off the church's giving; we live off *our* giving. It's a good day when we realize that! Another step of faith our people took at that time was deciding not to stop supporting ministries we were already supporting; in fact, we increased our giving to those ministries. Do you know what God did? It was the greatest year in my personal life, and it was the greatest year ever in the history of our church!

**WHEN GOD BLESSES US, HE HAS MORE THAN US IN MIND.**

We can never outgive God. And we are never more like Him than when we are generous.

I love the story about a little boy and his mom who enter a country store. The storekeeper tells the boy to reach into a bowl of lollipops on the counter. The little boy won't reach in there, so the storekeeper reaches in the bowl, grabs a handful of lollipops, and gives them to the boy. When the boy and his mom leave, she asks him why he wouldn't reach into the bowl for a lollipop. The boy says, "Well, Mom, the storekeeper has a bigger hand than I have!" We need to realize that God has a bigger hand than we do. As Jesus taught, "Give, and it will be given to you" (Luke 6:38).

Why is generosity important to leadership? When we are generous, we are depending on God and giving Him rule in our lives. Everything that God controls, gives. The sun gives heat, the moon gives light, and plants give food. Giving helps me reflect on God more in my daily walk.

Generosity is also a way to express gratitude to God. In John 12, a woman named Mary bought expensive perfume, equivalent to a year's wages—and poured it on Jesus' hair and feet. Judas got upset and considered her act of devotion a waste of money. I did not always understand this story until the Lord showed me something: Earlier, Jesus had raised Mary's brother, Lazarus, from the dead. Her generous actions were saying, "After what the Lord has done by bringing my brother back to life, this offering is no great sacrifice. It is my worship and my gratitude to Him."

**WE ARE NEVER MORE LIKE HIM THAN WHEN WE ARE GENEROUS.**

Giving is one way I can express my gratitude to God. If God never does one more thing for me other than save me, He has done enough, and I will praise Him for it! As the psalmist wrote, "Bless the LORD, O my soul, and all that is within me, bless his holy name! Bless the LORD, O my soul, and forget not all his benefits, who forgives all your iniquity, who heals all your diseases" (Ps. 103:1–3).

I want to bless and praise Him for all He has done and

is still doing for me. Giving is a way to express my gratitude to the Lord.

Another benefit of generosity is that it breaks the grip of materialism. The way to overcome greed is to be generous. When I was a boy, people used to tell me that I was so much like my uncle. I didn't want to be like my uncle because I saw how stingy he was. Even when I had no money, I decided I did not want to be stingy like him. Eventually he died and I preached his funeral. Afterward, I went to his wife's house. My uncle had done well financially; he was a miser, but he had done well. His wife told me that day, "I loved your uncle, and we were together a long time. But you know, we never went out and had a nice meal. I wanted to go out to a nice restaurant on my birthday or an anniversary, but we never went. We never took a vacation or had a memorable, enjoyable experience because of the way he lived so miserly."

**GENEROSITY BREAKS THE GRIP OF MATERIALISM AND ENABLES YOU TO BE MORE LIKE JESUS.**

Sometimes, we leaders have a disease that I call "sclerosis of the *giver*." In the guise of stewardship, leaders can sometimes become tightfisted with their family, staff, friends, and resources, which only hinders God from blessing their leadership efforts. But I believe that if you are materialistic or greedy, you can break the cycle by being generous to others. You can be generous with gifts of time, talent, money, gifts, and prayer. Generosity breaks the grip of materialism and enables you to be more like Jesus.

We should also be generous because it strengthens our faith. There is only one time in the entire Word of God where He tells us to put Him to the test, and that's in Malachi 3:10: "And thereby *put me to the test*, says the LORD of hosts, if I will not open the windows of heaven for you and pour down for you a blessing until there is no more need" (emphasis added). What this means to us is, God will use generosity and finances to build your faith more than anything else. Just start giving what you're able to give. Then give a little more. Keep growing your giving and watch what happens.

A tithe is a floor to your generosity, but it should not be a roof. When Barbara and I first came to Rock Springs Church, we were tithers as we are today. Our salary was a mere two hundred dollars per week, but we still tithed to the church. We were not making enough money for anything above our monthly bills. Then Barbara got sick and needed to go to the doctor. We really didn't know how we were going to pay the bill. When she returned home, she told me, "You are not going to believe what happened!" Dr. Lee Woodall was our doctor, and after he treated Barbara, he asked her to come into his office. He told her that his daddy was a pastor, and he was raised in a pastor's home. He had a heart for pastors, and he treated her that day at no cost.

Our church takes a Manger Offering each December in which the congregation can give to special projects going on around our church. One particular year, Barbara and I had been saving up to have dental work done. Barbara had taken medications while she endured seizures that God miraculously healed, and those medications had caused major damage to her teeth. I also had dental issues that needed to be addressed. No one knew about these needs; we were just saving for them privately.

As we were praying about what God wanted us to give

to the Manger Offering, I remember praying, "Lord, I am doing all I can do." He said to me, "That is your problem. You are looking at what you can do instead of what I can do." I told Him I loved Him; He told me to double our Manger Offering. Which meant we would need to use the money we were saving for dental work to give to the special offering.

So Barbara and I doubled our gift. After church the following Sunday night, after everyone else had left, three women stood waiting for me. They told me they worked for a dentist in Griffin, Georgia, and every year their office votes on one family to help with all their dental needs for a year. Their office voted for the Tate family that year.

God has built my faith more through giving than in any other way.

## FOR REFLECTION

1. What one thing stood out to you most in this chapter?

2. How do you currently practice generosity? In what ways can you step up your generosity?

3. In what areas of your life are you completely dependent on God? How has your faith grown by being dependent on God?

4. Share a time when you were a recipient of someone else's generosity. How did you feel?

5. What is one small way you can be generous today?

## PRINCIPLES TO REMEMBER

- Good leaders practice generosity.
- You cannot outgive God.
- Generosity is a way to express gratitude to God.
- Generosity breaks the grip of materialism and greed.
- Generosity strengthens your faith.

CHAPTER 20

# YES, TESTING CAN AFFIRM YOUR CALL TO LEAD

IN THIS BOOK we've examined simple, practical ways to lead others where you are right now, no matter who you are. But we all know that leading is not easy. When we understand why seasons and situations are hard, it can be easier to get through those challenging times.

Jesus teaches us so much about leadership. One of the things we see in His life is that when He chooses leaders, He puts them through tests. Jesus did not choose the most likely; He chose people no one else would have selected. He didn't go to the temple or the Sanhedrin to recruit leaders. He was not even in Jerusalem then—He was at the Sea of Galilee! Among others, Jesus chose seven fishermen. All these fishermen had ever done was fish! But He would use them to take His message to the ends of the world.

## THE ACTION TEST

We read in Luke 5:1–11 that Jesus borrowed a boat so He could teach the multitudes on the shore. This was Simon's boat. When Jesus finished speaking, He told Simon (soon to be named Peter) to launch out and let down his nets. Simon Peter replied that they had already fished all night and caught nothing, but he cast his net anyway. Immediately the nets were filled with fish and the nets broke. When Simon came to shore and saw Jesus, he fell at His feet. With Simon were James and John, brothers. Jesus commissioned them too to be fishers of men. Jesus had put them to the action test, they passed, and He called them to be His disciples.

**THE ONES JESUS CAN USE ARE WILLING TO MOVE PAST THE STATUS QUO.**

When He calls us to lead, we can expect tests. Most likely not fishing tests, but contemporary tests of our willingness to take bold steps and follow Him.

God often uses people who are willing to make bold moves. Will Rogers said, "Even if you are on the right track, you'll get run over if you just sit there."[1] You need to be willing to launch out into the deep. Remember this saying, "Things may come to those who wait, but only the things left by those who hustle."

The ones Jesus can use are willing to move past the status quo.

In my own life, I have always thought God had more for me, so I would do things that were not conventional to most. When other preachers were not in full-time ministry, I went into full-time ministry. I was from an area where most preachers didn't get an education, but I took college courses. I remember it was not easy to leave what was familiar. We left our family, our home, and everything comfortable to come to Georgia and pastor. That was my action test. He may give you an action test too. You may say you don't want to go out on a limb, but I will tell you that you will never taste the fruit if you refuse to go out on that limb.

## THE AUTHORITY TEST

The second test I see in Luke 5 is the authority test. Jesus said to Peter, James, and John, "Put out into the deep." These three fishermen knew the Sea of Galilee. They knew that its deepest point was 141 feet. They knew the fish were in the shallow water. To fish in this body of water you didn't go to the deep water, you went to the shallow water. It would have been quite natural for them to correct Jesus. Action people often struggle with the authority test. But when Jesus told them to take the boat into the deep, they did what they were told. Here's what the authority test teaches us: We will never be good leaders until we are good followers.

If serving is beneath you, leading will always be above you. The authority test is about serving and honoring those above you. To test our ability to respect authority, God may put us under leaders we don't always agree with.

In late 2023, there was a split between our main church campus and our Macon, Georgia, campus. Its cause was a misunderstanding of authority, which led to disunity. Sadly, people left the church. Since then, our current staff have done incredible work to rebuild both congregations and reestablish unity. The following year, a large church in the Macon area voted to merge with our church and become the new location for our Macon campus! God would not have been able to bless us like this in 2023 because we were not a unified body. God uses the benchmark of authority so His people can remain unified and there is order instead of chaos.

> **WE WILL NEVER BE GOOD LEADERS UNTIL WE ARE GOOD FOLLOWERS.**

The same is true in marriage. God cannot fully bless a

marriage if the couple is not unified and misunderstands authority in marriage. When we seek the blessing of God on our leadership, we need to be sure we are seeking unity with those we lead as well as those we follow. It is a beautiful testimony when we dwell together in unity: "Behold, how good and pleasant it is when brothers dwell in unity" (Psalm 133:1). You dwell in unity when you honor and respect those in authority in your life. If you don't regard your leaders with respect, you are not under God's will and are in danger of missing His blessing. Your leaders may not be the best or the brightest, but for this moment in time they are your authority, and God blesses those who honor and support those above them.

When I was a teenager, I ran a milling machine. I knew that the machine needed time to warm up before it ran. One day my boss came up and told me to run the machine right away. I tried to tell him that if the machine did not warm up it would jump into gear, break the cutter, and damage the part I was working on. Regardless, he ordered me to start the machine, which promptly busted and messed everything up. He was my authority, so I did what he said.

When someone in authority tells you something to do, you will be blessed by respecting and obeying that authority. If I want God to honor me, I need to honor His authority over my life. And He has placed me under the authority of the denomination of our church. I am under the authority of a board at my church. I am under the authority of a budget.

If you are unwilling to be under authority, you cannot do a respectable job leading those under your own authority.

## The Acknowledgment Test

A third test Jesus uses for potential leaders is the acknowledgment test. We read in Luke 5:6, "And when they had done this, they enclosed a large number of fish, and their nets were breaking." When Peter, James, and John let down the nets, the fish swarmed in from Crappie Corner, Bass Boulevard, and Lobster Lane.

"But when Simon Peter saw it, he fell at Jesus' knees, saying, 'Depart from me, for I am a sinful man, O Lord.' For he and all who were with him were astonished at the catch of fish that they had taken" (vv. 8–9). This is so good! When those nets started filling up, it would have been easy for Peter to say, "Look what I've done!" Instead, he confessed, "I am a sinful man."

Jesus is looking for us to acknowledge His work in our lives. We serve God until He gets the glory and somebody else gets the credit. I have a plaque at home with a quote from Ronald Reagan: "There is no limit to the amount of good you can do if you don't care who gets the credit."[2] We need to remember that we are flawed humans and when anything good happens under our leadership, it is God working through us. Everything good comes from Him. If we want to be the best leaders where God has us right now, we will acknowledge Him in every success we encounter. That's the acknowledgment test.

## The Abandonment Test

The fourth test is the abandonment test. Luke 5:11 says, "And when they had brought their boats to land, they left everything and followed him." The fishermen left their families, they left the familiar, and they left their fish to follow Jesus. Every leader God uses will be asked to abandon some things. God asked Abraham to leave his family in Ur to follow God to the promised land. God allowed Joseph to be sold into slavery and taken to Egypt. Jim Elliot said, "He is no fool who gives what he cannot keep to gain that which he cannot lose."[3] As a leader, you will likely have to consider abandoning what's familiar and comfortable to realize God's best for your life.

When I look back over our last thirty-five years at Rock Springs Church, I can see all the blessings we would have missed had we chosen not to leave what was comfortable and familiar to us. Jesus will sometimes ask us to abandon the "good" to discover His "best."

## The Anticipation Test

The fifth test is the anticipation test. "And when he had finished speaking, he said to Simon, 'Put out into the deep and let down your nets for a catch.' And Simon answered, 'Master, we toiled all night and took nothing! But at your word I will let down the nets'" (Luke 5:4–5). Simon's sense of anticipation wasn't much at the moment, but nevertheless he obeyed.

I have learned that many people, including some leaders, don't have an abundance mindset. People believe there is only one pie, and they must focus on getting pieces of the pie. As leaders, we should focus on how to make more pies. We shouldn't look at our situation and say we cannot accomplish something because we don't have enough people. We *find* the people, either new hires or contract workers. Good leaders don't sit around moaning that they don't have enough resources. They *find* enough resources.

## Yes, Testing Can Affirm Your Call to Lead

Good leaders don't say they are out of ideas—there are *always* more ideas.

Are you going to live and lead with an abundance mindset or a scarcity mindset? The fishermen had labored in vain all night and had a scarcity mindset. But Jesus would quickly change that!

As D. L. Moody said, "If God is your partner, make your plans *big*!"[4] Set aside a scarcity mindset and believe God can do big things.

When I first got to Rock Springs Church years ago, the baptistry was full of Christmas decorations. I removed the decorations only to find four inches of putrid mud at the bottom of the baptistry. No one had been baptized there in years! I pulled on my shorts, I shoveled, and I scrubbed. When the congregation came to church Wednesday night, some asked about the new, "weird" smell. I told them it may be Ajax, Comet, or Pine Sol. I said we were going to be baptizing people. I anticipated God doing big things, and I wanted to be ready.

In 2024, Rock Springs Church led more than twenty seven hundred people to Christ. Indeed, God has done *great* things!

You must give up to go up. The fishermen had to let go of fishing. To do something big for God, you may have to let go of something that's familiar and comfortable.

Before Jesus chose His disciples He gave them tests. If life is hard for you right now, it may be a test to see if you're fit for the next thing God has in store for you. God allowed Joseph to be tested in the pit. God allowed Joseph to be tested in Potiphar's house. And God allowed Joseph to be tested in prison before He ever put Him in the palace.

Yes, God's tests can affirm your calling!

## FOR REFLECTION

1. Why do you believe Jesus would choose you to be a leader for Him?

2. What are you willing to surrender to do what God has called you to? Will this surrender be a sacrifice?

3. Who are the people you report to? How are you doing when it comes to respecting and honoring their authority?

4. How are you anticipating God to move in a big way in your life? Could you ask Him for more? How are you trusting Him to do exceedingly and abundantly?

## PRINCIPLES TO REMEMBER

- Leaders are often put through seasons of testing.
- We should embrace God's tests by trusting Him and doing what He tells us to do.
- Leaders are often called to abandon the familiar and comfortable in order to follow God's better path for their lives.
- We should respect authority and submit to those God has placed in leadership over us.
- A good leader anticipates that God will move in *big* ways.

## CONCLUSION
# DOES LEADERSHIP REALLY MATTER?

YES, LEADERSHIP MATTERS. The principles in this book come from a man who has lived them. I have seen what has worked and what has not. I've observed leaders who have gone before me. I saw what was working for them, and I began doing those things. I've said this before, and I'll say it again: Monkey see, monkey do. I am praying that this book will help influence you to step up and be a good leader.

We all get to choose who we look to for leadership examples.

One of my first examples of positive leadership was Spud Powers. He and I worked at the car lot for my stepdad, making fifty dollars per week. Spud was not treated very well; my stepdad didn't treat either of us very well. Anyway, I would be in the back filling up boxes as I was told, and Spud would come back and help me. Spud would also walk me around the lot and teach me about the cars. In my life, nobody had ever spent time with me like Spud. The adults in my life hardly even came to watch me in sports, and we certainly did not go watch sports together.

One of my favorite activities at the time was to listen to Warren County football on the radio on Friday nights. I knew I would never get to go. But one day, Spud asked my mama, "Melba, can I take Benny with me to the football game?" She said, "I guess." I remember watching the Warren County Pioneers that night and it felt like the Super Bowl! Despite his modest position at the car lot, Spud was a leader to me. "Benny, let me help you fill those boxes." Or "Benny, come out here on the car lot with me." Or "Benny, come with me to the football game." Spud Powers wanted to spend time with me. My stepdad had the position, but Spud influenced me. I looked up to him. I learned that leadership was about influence and care.

Paul said in 1 Corinthians 11:1, "Be imitators of me, as I am of Christ." We must remember that if we are leaders, we should be looking to Jesus as our ultimate example. Jesus served us all with nail-scarred hands. Jesus cared about and influenced masses of people. We see His compassion for the hurting, blind, and lame. We see Jesus inspire people to follow Him, and the result is the world coming to know His name as the Savior of the world!

Like Jesus, our motivation to lead should be to glorify God in all we do. In Nehemiah 6:15–16 we read, "So the wall was finished on the twenty-fifth day of the month Elul, in fifty-two days. And when all our enemies heard of it, all the nations around us were afraid and fell greatly in their own esteem, for they perceived that *this work had been accomplished with the help of our God*" (emphasis added).

Does leadership matter? Absolutely! Leadership is seeing value in people, recognizing each person as an individual, caring for them, and being a positive influence in their lives.

I would like to conclude by telling you where I learned about caring for people. When I started in the ministry, there was a successful preacher named Charles "Cotton" Ross who had a large church. People were giving their lives to Christ in his church. As a young preacher, I would ask Cotton if I could go on hospital visits with him. On one of these visits I asked, "What is it about your church that brings people? You have such growth!" Cotton told me, "Benny, it is caring for the people. I love my people. I pray for my people. I visit them in the hospital. I provide care for my people." Cotton was not a great orator, but his ministry was reaching so many.

**MAKE HEAVEN BIGGER BY CARING BETTER.**

His secret sauce? Caring for people. Because of Cotton's influence in my life, Rock Springs Church developed this vision statement: "Make heaven bigger by caring better."

If you were to visit me and sit in my office, I would tell you that you are in the people business. As a leader, if you lose sight of the fact that you're in the people business, you have lost. Look for ways to connect with people. Care for the people and you will lead at your best.

I'm here to tell you that if God can use Benny Tate to lead a family and Rock Springs Church, He certainly can use you! By following Jesus and leading at our best, we are laborers with God and can influence those around us. If we care for people, everything else takes care of itself. My prayer for you is that as you care for others with the heart of Jesus, others will want to know more about Him. Indeed you can make heaven bigger by caring better.

# A PERSONAL INVITATION FROM THE AUTHOR

FRIEND, GOD LOVES you deeply. His Word is filled with promises that reveal His desire to bring healing, hope, and abundant life to every area of your body, mind, and spirit. More than anything, He wants a personal relationship with you through His Son, Jesus Christ.

If you've never invited Jesus into your life, you can do so right now. It's not about religion—it's about a relationship with the One who knows you completely and loves you unconditionally. If you're ready to take that step, do not wait one more second. Simply pray this prayer and ask Jesus into your life:

> *Lord Jesus, I am a sinner, and I am sorry for my sins. I'm so sorry that I want to change. I believe You died on the cross as payment for my sins. I confess my sins to You right now. Come into my heart, Lord. Come into my life and forgive me. Thank You, Jesus, for forgiving me. Thank You for saving me!*

If you just prayed that prayer, congratulations! You've made the most important decision of your life. Your sins are forgiven, and you are now part of the family of God. I encourage you to tell a pastor at your church so they can help you with your next steps as a believer. I also invite you to scan the following Flowcode or visit MadeNew.info to access several resources that will help you grow in your walk with Jesus.

# APPENDIX
# SPIRITUAL GIFTS TEST

I F YOU ARE interested in discovering your spiritual gifts, visit www.giftstest.com or www.spiritualgiftstest.com to take an assessment. Once you identify your spiritual gifts, continue learning more about your gifts and seek opportunities to use them. If you are not already involved in a local church, I encourage you to get involved and seek ways to serve within the congregation using your spiritual gifts!

# ACKNOWLEDGMENTS

I WANT TO EXTEND a special thank you to my precious wife, Barbara. Our marriage of four decades has been a kingdom marriage! Your support and prayer have been the wind beneath my wings for everything I have attempted and accomplished.

Thank you to Stacey Hensley! The sacrifice you have given in every way to this project is unparalleled. I simply do not have the words to express my gratitude to you and Mike. I love, respect, and admire you both deeply. Thank you from the bottom of my heart. There is no book without you!

Thank you to our communications director, Amy Varner, and my administrative assistant, Abbey Shiflett. You both helped make this a reality. Thank you to my Rock Springs staff! You are America's best. Everything in this book, I first taught you! Thanks for being the guinea pig! I love all of you!

Rock Springs Church, thank you for allowing me to have the high honor of serving as your pastor for thirty-five years. There is no other place anywhere near this place, like this place, so this must be the place! There is nowhere like Rock Springs. I love you!

Thank you, Charisma House. Your experience and partnership took this book to another level. I have worked with publishers before, but you are simply the best.

Lastly, and most importantly, I want to thank Jesus Christ. Everything I know about leadership, I learned from Jesus. To Him be all the glory, honor, and praise. Yes, to God be the glory, to the people be the credit, and the privilege has been mine!

# NOTES

### Chapter 1

1. Bible Hub, "*kol,*" accessed July 2, 2025, https://biblehub.com/hebrew/3605.htm.

### Chapter 2

1. "Abraham Lincoln," Our Lost Founding, accessed July 9, 2025, http://www.ourlostfounding.com/national-day-of-prayer-upon-my-knees/

### Chapter 3

1. "Abraham Lincoln," Goodreads, accessed July 4, 2025, https://www.goodreads.com/quotes/10466454-discipline-is-choosing-between-what-you-want-now-and-what.

### Chapter 5

1. "Albert Schweitzer," BrainyQuote, accessed July 9, 2025, https://www.brainyquote.com/quotes/albert_schweitzer_133001.
2. "Howard G. Hendricks," AZ Quotes, July 4, 2025, https://www.azquotes.com/quote/544235.

### Chapter 6

1. "Maya Angelou," Goodreads, accessed July 9, 2025, https://www.goodreads.com/quotes/5934-i-ve-learned-that-people-will-forget-what-you-said-people.

### Chapter 7

1. "Others" by Charles D. Meigs, Library of Timeless Truths, accessed July 6, 2025, https://www.library.timelesstruths.org/music/others.
2. Mary Kay Ash," Brainy Quotes, accessed July 9, 2025, https://www.brainyquote.com/quotes/mary-kay-ash-393052.

## Chapter 8

1. "Martin Luther," Goodreads, accessed July 6, 2025, https://www.goodreads.com/quotes/870042-god-made-man-out-of-nothing-and-as-long-as.
2. "The Indispensable Man," Blowing Away My Life, accessed July 9, 2025, https://www.blowingawaymylife.wordpress.com/2012//06/15/the-indispensable-man/.

## Chapter 9

1. "William James Quotes," AZ Quotes, accessed July 8, 2025, https://www.azquotes.com/author/7341-William_James.
2. "Who's Your Daddy," Mountain Wings, accessed July 8, 2024, https://www.mountainwings.com/past/2361.htm.

## Chapter 10

1. "When it's foggy in the pulpit, it's cloudy in the pew," AllGreatQuotes, accessed July 7, 2025, https://www.allgreatquotes.com/quote-88785/.
2. Bible Hub, "oracle," accessed July 7, 2025, https://biblehub.com/hebrew/4853.htm.

## Chapter 12

1. Marcia Dunn, "Apollo 11 Moon Landing Had Thousands Working Behind Scenes," Associated Press, July 15, 2019, https://apnews.com/article/70fb09bc207a4dc1a917f3a5aa9ed86e.

## Chapter 13

1. "Billy Graham and Jim Bakker's Lowest Moment—Full Story," posted on February 28, 2018, by *The Jim Bakker Show*, YouTube, https://www.youtube.com/watch?v=xsywV-cjifg&t=66s.

## Chapter 15

1. "Whitfield and Wesley," Bible.org, accessed July 8, 2025, https://bible.org/illustration/whitfield-and-wesley; Warren W. Wiersbe and Lloyd M. Perry, *Wycliffe Handbook of Preaching and Preachers* (Moody Press, 1984), 255.

*Notes*

2. "John Wesley's Diary," Southport United Methodist Church, October 26, 2023, https://sumc.org/blog/john-wesleys-diary/.
3. "Paul Harvey," AZ Quotes, accessed August 11, 2025, https://www.azquotes.com/quote/815058.
4. "Quote by Vance Havner," Grace Quotes, accessed July 9, 2025, https://gracequotes.org/author-quote/vance-havner/.

### CHAPTER 17

1. A. W. Tozer, *The Root of the Righteous* (Wing Spread Publishers, 1986), 34.

### CHAPTER 18

1. "Ralph Waldo Emerson," Goodreads, accessed July 9, 2025, https://www.goodreads.com/quotes/8468-in-my-walks-every-man-i-meet-is-my-superior.
2. "Larry King," Goodreads, accessed July 9, 2025, https://www.goodreads.com/author/quotes/19874.larry_king.
3. "Babe Ruth," BrainyQuote, accessed July 9, 2025, https://www.brainyquote.com/quotes/babe_ruth_378138.

### CHAPTER 20

1. "Will Rogers," Goodreads, accessed July 9, 2025, https://www.goodreads.com/quotes/23961-even-if-you-are-on-the-right-track-you-ll-get.
2. "Ronald Reagan, "Goodreads, accessed July 9, 2025, https://www.goodreads.com/quotes/29359-there-is-no-limit-to-the-amount-of-good-you.
3. Elisabeth Elliot, ed., *The Journals of Jim Elliot* (Revell, 1978).
4. "D. L. Moody," AZ Quotes, accessed July 9, 2025, https://www.azquotes.com/quote/523866.

# ABOUT THE AUTHOR

BENNY TATE HAS served as senior pastor of Rock Springs Church in Milner, Georgia, since 1990. Under his leadership, the congregation has grown from eighty to more than eight thousand people. Tate served as president of the Congregational Methodist denomination for ten years and has served as the chaplain for the United States Senate and House of Representatives. He is the author of *Defy the Odds* and host of the *Leads Club* podcast. Tate and his wife, Barbara, have been married since 1984 and have one daughter, Savannah Abigail Tate.